D. J. Vickery MA MEd

Brodie's Notes on Peter Shaffer's

The Royal Hunt
of the Sun

Pan Books London and Sydney

First published 1978 by Pan Books Ltd
Cavaye Place, London SW10 9PG
2 3 4 5 6 7 8 9
© D. J. Vickery 1978
ISBN 0 330 50125 9
Filmset in Great Britain by
Northumberland Press Ltd, Gateshead, Tyne and Wear
Printed and bound by
Richard Clay (The Chaucer Press) Ltd, Bungay, Suffolk

Contents

Page references in these Notes are to the Pan edition of
Plays of the Sixties, Volume One, but as references are also
given to particular Acts and Scenes, the Notes may be
used with any edition of the play.

To the student

A close reading of the play is the student's primary task —
but it is well worth while seeing a performance if possible.
These notes will help to increase your understanding and
appreciation of the play, and to stimulate *your own* thinking
about it: *they are in no way intended as a substitute* for a
thorough knowledge of the play.

You will also be helped to a greater understanding of
Shaffer and his work by reading as many as possible of his
other plays (see 'The author and his work', pp.8–10); and
the books listed as 'Recommended reading' on p.10.

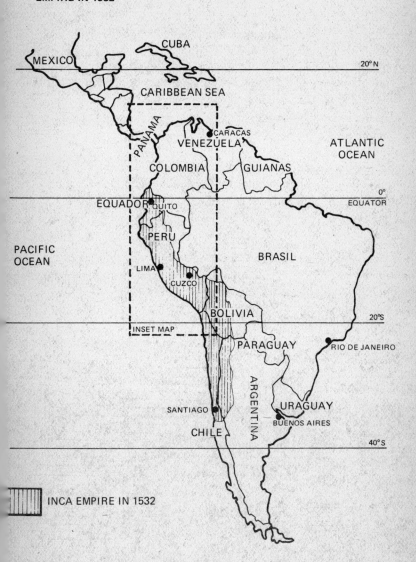

A MAP OF CENTRAL AND SOUTH AMERICA
SHOWING MODERN STATE BOUNDARIES AND
THE APPROXIMATE EXTENT OF THE INCA
EMPIRE IN 1532

INCA EMPIRE IN 1532

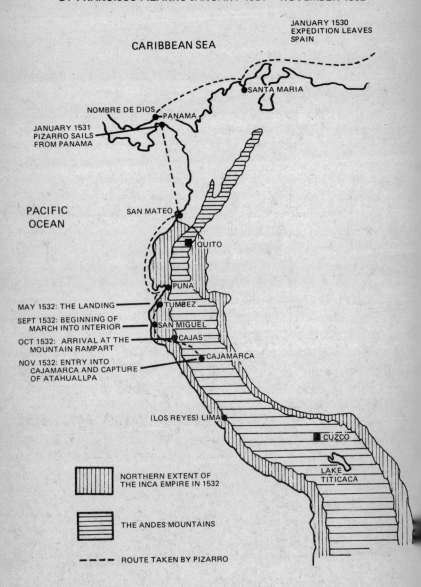

A DETAILED MAP OF THE NORTHERN EXTENT OF
THE INCA EMPIRE IN 1532 AND THE ROUTE TAKEN
BY FRANCISCO PIZARRO JANUARY 1531 – NOVEMBER 1532

JANUARY 1530
EXPEDITION LEAVES
SPAIN

CARIBBEAN SEA

SANTA MARIA

NOMBRE DE DIOS

PANAMA

JANUARY 1531
PIZARRO SAILS
FROM PANAMA

PACIFIC
OCEAN

SAN MATEO

QUITO

PUNA

MAY 1532: THE LANDING

TUMBEZ

SEPT 1532: BEGINNING OF
MARCH INTO INTERIOR

SAN MIGUEL

OCT 1532: ARRIVAL AT THE
MOUNTAIN RAMPART

CAJAS

CAJAMARCA

NOV 1532: ENTRY INTO
CAJAMARCA AND CAPTURE
OF ATAHUALLPA

(LOS REYES) LIMA

CUZCO

LAKE
TITICACA

NORTHERN EXTENT OF
THE INCA EMPIRE IN 1532

THE ANDES MOUNTAINS

– – – – ROUTE TAKEN BY PIZARRO

Foreword

We are fortunate that several of Francisco Pizarro's companions on his conquest of Peru set themselves up as chroniclers to provide a fascinating series of eye-witness accounts which later historians have drawn upon extensively. The disadvantage of such a wide range of personal documentation lies in the variation in historical accuracy which inevitably accompanies such subjective accounts.

The most notable divergences are to be found in recorded dates, though there is rarely a difference of more than a few days. Thus the time of Pizarro's sailing from Panama varies from 27 December 1530 to 3 January 1531, while the capture of Cajamarca is variously set at 15 November and 16 November 1532. The greatest divergence in dates can be distinguished in the day on which Atahuallpa was executed; John Hemming places his death on Saturday, 26 July, while Jean Descola prefers Friday, 29 August 1533 – a gap of more than four weeks. Other, though less significant differences in the chronicles of events relate to the spelling of the names of places and characters and the exact complement of Pizarro's force.

As far as possible this Study Aid follows the dates and spellings employed by Peter Shaffer, who appears to have used as the primary source for his play William Prescott's *History of the Conquest of Peru*.

The author and his work

Peter Shaffer belongs to that generation of playwrights, born in the late 1920s and early 1930s, whose work began to appear on the London stage towards the end of the fifties, and is often collectively referred to as the New Drama. Whereas many of his contemporaries, notably John Osborne and Harold Pinter, appeared to burst upon the theatrical scene with plays of stunning and shocking innovation, Shaffer's origins in dramatic literature were extremely conventional and it was only after a period of lengthy experimentation that his creative originality as an artist began to make itself evident. In the case of nearly all the other writers of the New Drama it is the individual quality of their work that engages the interest and attention, but one of the most intriguing aspects of Shaffer's writing is its impersonality. This is not to say that he is as enigmatic as a Beckett or Stoppard, but he has been consistently concerned that his plays should be judged in their own right as works of art uninfluenced by psychological observations upon their author.

Born in London in 1926, one of twin brothers (his twin, Antony Shaffer, was the author of the successful West End thriller *Sleuth*), Shaffer worked as a coal miner (1944–7) before proceeding to Trinity College, Cambridge. Here he took his degree and began writing detective novels in collaboration with his brother, and experimenting with plays. After Cambridge he worked for a time as a librarian in New York, but his literary career began as a dramatist for television with the production of *The Salt Land* (1955) and *Balance of Terror* (1957). Recognition came with *Five Finger Exercise* (1958), on the surface a traditional drawing-room drama set among a middle-class Suffolk family. The play, however, merits Shaffer's inclusion among the New Dramatists by its penetrating psychological exposure of the conflicts and tensions that underlie the apparently stable family. The work won the *Evening Standard* Award for the best play of the year, and was followed in 1962 by *The Private Ear* and *The Public Eye*, two one-act plays comprising a double bill. The surprise expressed by some critics at the relatively lightweight nature of these two pieces was answered by *The Royal Hunt of the Sun*, which Shaffer had been working on for a considerable time before its appearance on stage in 1964. The play remains Shaffer's most ambitious work, though some have found its language and imagery inadequate for the bold, non-naturalistic style, and it marks a radical technical departure in its full-scale historical treatment of the conquest of Peru.

The play was originally intended for the Royal Shakespeare Company, but its directors seem to have been daunted by the magnitude of the production and size of the cast, and after some further re-writing (each draft gaining in clarity and simplicity compared with its forerunner) it was accepted by the National Theatre to become one of its most remarkable popular successes. First performed on 7 July 1964 at the Chichester Festival Theatre, the play later transferred to the London Old Vic with Colin Blakely as Pizarro and Robert Stephens as Atahuallpa. In 1969 a film version was produced with Robert Shaw as Francisco Pizarro, and Christopher Plummer as the Inca.

This *tour de force* was followed a year later by another one-act play in the earlier naturalistic mode, of extraordinary inventiveness but based on an idea of dazzling simplicity. By reversing the normal theatrical conventions of light and dark, *Black Comedy* (1965) represents one of the most ingenious farces written this century. Shaffer's next two plays written for the theatre were largely unsuccessful. *The White Liars* (1968) did reach the stage in New York and London in two different versions, but *The Battle of Shrivings* (1970) has yet to achieve a major professional performance, and has only recently been published in a revised version. A significant feature, however, of even the first version of *Shrivings* is the appearance of ideas derived from the psychologist R. D. Laing. In *Equus* (1973) Laing's theories receive coherent expression as the basis for a shocking and mysterious crime – the blinding of a number of horses by a boy who has been their worshipper – which is shaped, by means of dramatic ritual and an eloquent text, into the most complete theatrical experience of Shaffer's creation.

Recommended reading

The Conquest of the Incas, J. Hemming (Macmillan)

History of the Conquest of Peru, W. Prescott (Everyman's Library)

Peter Shaffer, J. R. Taylor (Longmans)

The play's historical background

The Spaniards

In 1492 Christopher Columbus set sail westwards into the Atlantic to begin a period of intense Spanish exploration and conquest in the Caribbean and the northern coasts of South America. A sensational early success was achieved in 1519 when Hernan Cortez discovered and invaded the powerful Aztec empire of Mexico and with little more than five hundred men and a few horses conquered an exotic and wealthy empire of over ten million inhabitants. Cortez's achievement fired the imaginations of many young Spaniards eager to gain fortunes and adventure on the far side of the Atlantic.

In the vanguard of the Spanish venturers was Francisco Pizarro, a senior officer in the expedition under Vasco Nunez de Balboa which broke through the forests of Panama to discover the Pacific Ocean in 1513. Pizarro subsequently commanded two expeditions in 1524 and 1527 down the coast of modern Colombia in search of an advanced civilization believed to lie in the south; his perseverance was rewarded when, in 1528, his force caught sight of its first Inca city at Tumbez. Realizing the magnitude of their discovery but unable to impress the governor of Panama with even the sophisticated evidence they brought back, the explorers decided to send Pizarro back to Spain to win royal approval and raise more men and money. He was fortunate that his visit coincided with the return of Cortez with a vast treasure from Mexico, and had little trouble recruiting young venturers in his home town (Shaffer's play begins here) and convincing the king. In Charles's absence, on 26 July 1529, the Queen signed the royal declaration authorizing Pizarro to discover and conquer Peru and naming him its Governor and Captain General.

Pizarro sailed from Seville in January 1530 and on reaching Panama lost no time in organizing his force for the return journey southwards. Sailing at the beginning of January 1531, Pizarro explored the coast of Ecuador before reaching Tumbez once more in early 1532. He was surprised to find the city in ruins and was informed by natives that the destruction was a result of a civil war within the Inca empire. Pizarro left Tumbez in May 1532 and advanced along the coast to San Miguel de Piura where he established the first Spanish settlement in this mysterious new country.

Leaving about sixty Spaniards as its first inhabitants, Pizarro marched out of San Miguel on 24 September 1532 with sixty-two horsemen and 106 foot soldiers and struck into the interior of the Inca empire. At the town of Cajas, also severely damaged in the recent civil war, Pizarro's force was met by an envoy from the victorious Atahuallpa with presents and an invitation to meet the Inca at Cajamarca, high in the mountains of the Andes. After a difficult and frightening climb the Spaniards reached the valley of Cajamarca on Friday, 15 November 1532.

Finding the Inca's army of over forty thousand troops spread out on a hillside beyond the town. Francisco Pizarro sent a party under Hernando de Soto, and including his brother Hernando Pizarro, to greet Atahuallpa and suggest a meeting. De Soto returned with a promise that Atahuallpa would visit Pizarro on the following day, and instructions for the Spanish force to make its quarters around the central square of the town.

Realizing that he had allowed his men to be led into a potential trap, Pizarro decided during the night that the only way of ensuring the safety of himself and his frightened and desperate force was to grasp the initiative and attempt to kidnap the head of state – a tactic that Cortez had used with devastating effect in the conquest of Mexico. Plans were therefore laid for a surprise attack and capture of the Inca during his visit to the town arranged for the next day.

At midday on Saturday, 16 November Atahuallpa moved towards the town with his Indian followers and attendants, all clothed in full ceremonial robes in an impressive show of power. The Spaniards waited, concealed in their buildings, while the Inca advanced so slowly that he did not reach the town square until late in the day. A Dominican Friar, Vincente de Valverde, approached to greet Atahuallpa and present the customary revelation of the nature of the Christian religion. When, however, the Inca angrily threw away a proffered prayer book, Pizarro decided to give the signal for attack, and the Spaniards charged their horses into the mass of unarmed natives. In the ensuing two hours, all that remained of daylight, an appalling carnage took place in which over six thousand Indians met their deaths and Atahuallpa was taken prisoner and placed in the temple of the sun at the edge of Cajamarca.

The next day Atahuallpa instructed his army to surrender without resistance, and immediately began to devise a way of extricating himself from the trap he had fallen into. Realizing that the Spaniards' main interest seemed to be in the precious metals his country could provide in plenty, he offered his famous ransom: a room filled, within the space of two months, with gold and twice over with silver, in exchange for his freedom and the prospect of restoration to his kingdom. Pizarro readily agreed to an offer of such amazing wealth, especially as he was also guaranteed time to send news of his success to Panama, and to muster reinforcements. Both sides settled down to await the outcome of events, with Atahuallpa an almost willing prisoner.

After an initial period of some delay, a steady trickle of treasure soon found its way to Cajamarca. Eager to complete his ransom as quickly as possible, Atahuallpa persuaded

Francisco Pizarro to send his brother Hernando to explore the riches of the temple at Pachacamac and ascertain the intentions of the powerful army commanded by Challcuchima, while envoys were despatched to speed up the flow of gold from Cuzco, the Inca capital. When Hernando Pizarro returned to Cajarmarca on 25 April 1533, he brought no gold but ample compensation in the person of Challcuchima, whose capture gave the Spaniards power over the military as well as the spiritual leader of the Inca empire.

Meanwhile, reinforcements had arrived from Panama under Diego de Almagro which almost doubled the Spanish force in the town and led the Inca to believe that his captors might never honour their agreement.

At the same time, the Spaniards began to suspect that Atahuallpa was secretly planning to be rescued by an army under his general Rumiñavi, and pressure was brought to bear on Francisco Pizarro to dispose of the captive who, many felt, had become more of a liability than a security. In an atmosphere of frenzied argument, Pizarro ordered the melting down and distribution of the gold and silver that had reached Cajamarca, and prepared to advance with the Inca to Cuzco. When however, news was brought of the imminent approach of a vast horde of native troops, an emergency meeting of the Spanish council was held in which Pizarro reluctantly agreed to the demands of his officers, and Atahuallpa was sentenced to death.

Once the decision had been taken, the Spaniards acted with frightening speed. Atahuallpa, having agreed at the last moment to receive baptism, was spared burning at the stake; and, on the evening of Friday, 29 August 1533, he was strangled by the rope in the square of Cajamarca. The next day the Inca was awarded the full ceremony of a Christian burial, which all the Spaniards attended.

The Incas

Inca Peru was the product of thousands of years of isolated development. It lay along the peaks of the Andes and the arid strip of coastal desert between the Andes and the Pacific. To the west lay the world's widest ocean, to the east the impenetrable barrier of the Amazon forests, and to the south the bleak expanses of Patagonia.

Empire

The Incas themselves had been an insignificant mountain tribe occupying only the valley of Cuzco, but after about 1200, when the first sovereign of the Incas, Manco-Capac, flourished, there began a period of conquest, first to the south and north and then in all directions. In about 1440, the Incas were attacked and almost overwhelmed by the neighbouring Chanca tribe, but defended themselves and won a major victory on the plain above Cuzco. This success heralded a period of vast and sudden expansion under Pachacuti (ruler from 1438 to 1471) and his son Topac Inca, who died in 1493. These two, according to a modern authority, rank with Alexander, Ghengis Khan and Napoleon among the world's 'great conquerors'. By means of a combination of military skill and administrative expertise they established an empire that stretched for nearly 4,828 km (about 3,000 miles) along the Andes from about the second degree north (in the south of modern Colombia) to the thirty-seventh degree of southern latitude (around the centre of modern Chile).

The conquest was both imperialistic and religious, though wherever possible the Incas avoided bloodshed, preferring to absorb tribes into the empire by attraction, gradually admitting defeated chiefs into their own privileged class and transplanting their own aristocrats into newly won areas. The religion of the sun was imposed on all that the Incas conquered, though the defeated were allowed to keep their respective dress, customs and certain religious observances that did not conflict with the cult of the sun.

When the first Spanish explorers reached the Pacific in the early sixteenth century the empire was ruled in peace and tranquillity by one venerated supreme Inca, Huayana-Capac.

Social Structure

The stability and prosperity achieved by Huayana-Capac was based on a system of rigid bureaucratic control (the Inca himself was absolute ruler, surrounded by an atmosphere of divinity which added more profound authority to his power). Members of the royal family occupied all important ministerial positions throughout the empire under him but at all times looked to the Inca for leadership. Immediately below them was the caste of Inca nobility, distinguished by the golden ornaments in their ears (which caused them to be nicknamed 'big-ears' by the Spanish), occupying the lesser governmental positions. Further down the managerial structure were minor officials and foremen, each of whom was responsible for ten ordinary citizens at the base of a vast administrative pyramid whose apex was the Inca himself.

The Incas ruled conscientiously but they also indulged in every available form of luxury and privilege, while members of the entire Inca tribe enjoyed special prestige and a feeling that they were part of an élite. A portion of all produce was set aside as taxes and skilled workmen were transferred to Cuzco to work for the Inca and the privileged nobility. Gold and silver were the prerogative of the Inca and overseers were appointed to the mines to see that none went into unauthorized hands.

The ordinary Peruvians lived simple peasant lives in what was a well ordered agricultural society. The Incas had applied their extraordinary organizational genius to overcome the geographical difficulties of their country, setting up agricultural collectives to build and maintain elaborate terraces and building a system of canals and underground aqueducts to fertilize the dry coastal plain. Storehouses full of food, and herds of llamas, were established as insurance against bad harvests, while the rural population was redistributed to equalize the standard of living throughout the empire.

Huayana-Capac and his royal predecessors had made a genuine effort to ensure the wellbeing and happiness of their subjects, and as a result of administrative efficiency and a stable regime of disciplined agricultural labour the population of the Inca empire flourished. The ordinary people formed a perfect labouring class, living collectively, with no private property, and strongly bound to their families and tribes, villages and fields. Furthermore, it was the object of the Incas to infuse their subjects with a spirit of passive obedience and a conservative acceptance of the established order of things; in this they fully succeeded.

'The Spaniards who first visited the country are emphatic in their testimony, that no government could have been better suited to the genius of the people; and no people could have appeared more contented with their lot, or more devoted to their government.'
William Prescott, *The Conquest of Peru*

Religion
Inca religion was a complex mixture of ceremonies, practices and beliefs drawn from a variety of tribes and clans whose underlying principle was the worship of nature culminating in the adoration of the sun.

The creator god of the Incas and pre-Incas was Viracocha, who gave life to the earth, man and animals. But it was to deities such as Apu Illapu (the rain-giver) and Mama-Kilya (Moon Mother, wife of the Sun god and protectress of women) that the common folk addressed their prayers. Supreme among all the gods and minor deities that the Inca peoples worshipped, however, was Inti, the sun god whose warmth embraced the earth of the Andes and matured crops. As the most powerful influence on men's lives, he was naturally beloved by farmers; portions of the land, whose produce supported the temples, were allotted to the sun and administered for the priests. A Festival of the Sun took place in June of each year, the purpose of which was to secure a good maize harvest and a renewal of the crops, as well as human health and strength.

The Sun Temple in Cuzco was the most magnificent of all Inca temples and contained an enormous image of the Inti represented as the oldest son of the creator god, as well as a special area within, containing solid golden models of a variety of agricultural items: cornstalks, llamas, even lumps of earth. The temple was entrusted to the chief priest Villac Umu, his assistants, and a convent of chosen women sworn to perpetual chastity in the service of the Inca.

The Sun God was considered to be the Inca's divine ancestor and frequently addressed as 'father' by the emperor, while the ruling Inca was looked upon as the sun incarnate and was thus often addressed as Inti. The deification and glorification of the Inca were essential props in the Incas' rule over their great empire, since the common people had unquestioning faith in their leader's omniscience, infallibility and immortality. Only the Inca and his immediate relatives, therefore, were aware that the claim for solar descent originated in an occasion when their ancestor Manco-Capac had used a suit of shining armour to reflect the sun's rays – an act perpetuated by means of the golden disc that reflected the sun's rays in the sun temple at Cuzco.

Civil War
While the Spanish explorers were making their first tentative probes southwards along the Pacific coast from Panama, the stability of the Inca empire was profoundly shaken when the

ruling emperor Huayana-Capac and his probable heir Ninan Cuyuchi both became victims of a mysterious fever at some time between 1525 and 1527. The premature deaths of the Inca and his successor left the empire in the hands of another son, Huascar, and his illegitimate brother, Atahuallpa. Atahuallpa had possession of the professional army, which had been fighting, under its generals Challcuchima, Quisquis and Rumiñavi, against rebellious tribes in the northern province around Quito. Huascar, on the other hand, while becoming ruler of the capital city Cuzco, had only the support of a reserve force of citizen soldiers. It took only a few years for relations between the two brothers to degenerate into open conflict. Huascar's militia attempted to invade Quito, but after initial successes was driven south through the Andes and suffered a crushing defeat in a pitched battle outside Quito.

It was the aftermath of the recent fighting in the northern province that Pizarro witnessed when he started his march down the coast of Peru. At the same time, a remarkable coincidence caused the victorious Atahuallpa to be encamped in the mountains at Cajamarca on his route from Quito to the capital city, where Huascar was being held captive by the triumphant Quisquis. Had Huayana-Capac been alive when the Spaniards set foot in Peru, they would almost certainly have been faced with a united resistance: only because the land was divided and unsettled by the wars of Huascar and Atahuallpa were they able to penetrate and conquer it. Thus Pizarro was fortunate to arrive at exactly the right moment, and the fruit of the empire for which the two brothers were reaching fell into the hands of the Spaniards.

We should also remember another factor that favoured the Spaniards: the natives' religious awe of the white men, whom they believed to be gods.

Dramatic influences, themes, style and language

Influences

While it is possible to identify similarities between Shaffer's ideas and the attitude that Shakespeare presents towards natural order and fame, there is a deep irony here in that – in Shakespeare's sense – Pizarro does achieve immortality, by living on in memory and history. The two most obvious influences on *The Royal Hunt of the Sun* are Kabuki Theatre and the work and ideas of Bertolt Brecht – especially those on epic theatre.

Kabuki is a type of Japanese theatre based on popular legends, myths and historical events (and therefore long and episodic) which makes use of elaborate scenery and costumes and in which the actors employ heavily conventionalized make-up. A reciter or narrator is used in many of its forms and the action is augmented by drums, flutes and a variety of musical instruments depending on the origin of the play being performed. Shaffer has acknowledged that he had this kind of non-realistic, ritualistic theatre in mind when he wrote *The Royal Hunt of the Sun*, and its conventions provide a valuable guideline to any visualization or production of the play.

Bertolt Brecht (1898–1956), the German poet, playwright and theatrical reformer has been one of the most important figures in 20th-century European drama, and has influenced the work of countless writers in addition to Peter Shaffer. The main impulse of Brecht's art is a violently anti-bourgeois attitude that reflects his generation's deep disappointment in the civilization (cf. Pizarro) that had collapsed after the First World War. His experiences in military service made him a lifelong pacifist and he expressed in his work the moral and political dilemmas of a mass society in which man is helpless and isolated. In the most creative period of his life he produced a series of deeply-felt poetic parables in which such fundamental issues as whether it is possible to be a good human being in a society based on greed (cf. Spain); and the impossibility of combining human kindness with efficiency as a capitalist identified by cruelty and selfishness and accompanied by the forces of chaos, sex, greed and violence. His 'Lehrstücke' (learning-pieces) demonstrated the hope that his discovery of Marxism had given a solution to the ills of mankind, and the difficulty of achieving justice in a wicked world.

The essence of Brecht's theory of drama is the idea that a truly Marxist drama must avoid making the audience believe in the presence of the actors on the stage: should not make it identify with them, but should rather follow the methods of the epic poet's art, which is to make the audience realize that what it sees on stage is merely an account of past events (cf. Old Martin's role) that it should watch with critical detachment. Hence the epic (narrative, non-dramatic) theatre is based on detachment, achieved through a number of devices that remind the spectator that he is being presented with a demonstration of human behaviour rather than an illusion of reality: 'in short, that the theatre is only a theatre and not the world itself'.

Themes

Many have said that the value or profundity of the play's philosophical ideas are less important as ideas than the brilliant visualization that complements and enriches the verbal debate. Even so, the complex pattern of thoughts and notions that define the characters and motivate their actions cannot be ignored, for they are of the play's essence.

At the heart of the play is the *search for God*, or rather a search for an individual definition of the idea of God. This

search motivates and inspires Pizarro and even provides Atahuallpa with the hope of confirming and ratifying his
acknowledged heritage. For those characters whose faith in
conventional Christian doctrine is established, the search is
for other forms of god. Young Martin worships at the altar of
his youthful hero Pizarro, in a way that is almost sacrilegious,
while Estete considers as profane any insults to his king –
the Holy Roman Emperor. For those who are tempted to
Peru purely by the thought of immense wealth, a material
form of god is their inspiration:

> Riches, the dumb god, that giv'st all men tongues,
> Thou canst do nought, and yet mak'st men do all things.
> B. Jonson – *Volpone* (I, 1)

The themes of *time* and *death* represent two inter-related philosophical problems, which have permeated a good deal of
modern drama – especially that of the Absurd. Pozzo's
famous lines from *Waiting for Godot* – 'They give birth astride
a grave, the light gleams an instant, then it's night once more'
– sum up the realization that for Pizarro ends any possibility
of experiencing the joy of existence. The ultimate truth in
life is the inevitability of death, and the relentless progress of
dying begins in the very moment of our being born. We may
for a while be distracted from this inescapable reality, but
from the moment we recognize it we are exiled from hope.
Time, therefore, which imprisons us between birth and
death, denies us a full awareness of ourselves, because the only
self we can conceive is compounded of memories accumulated by arbitrary selection from the past. Being subject to the
progress of time flowing through us and changing us in so
doing, we are, at no single moment in our lives, identical with
ourselves. The fascinating appeal of the Sun God for Pizarro
lies, therefore, in the fact that it is not only beyond time
(indeed it shapes time as far as the concept relates to the

pattern of men's lives) but is also beyond death, since it rises every day into new life.

The theme of *loyalty* also contributes significantly to the structure of ideas in *The Royal Hunt of the Sun*, and Peter Shaffer has emphasized its importance by saying: 'To me, the greatest tragic factor in history is man's apparent need to mark the intensity of his reaction to life by joining a band: for a band, to give itself definition, must find a rival or an enemy. The neurotic allegiances of Europe, the Churches and flags, the armies and parties, are the villains of *The Royal Hunt*. All the major characters in the play, with the exception of Pizarro and Atahuallpa, seek to justify their attitudes and actions by means of the loyalty they express to either the Church, the Crown or the Army and the dramatic tension of Act 2 Scene 10 derives from the pressure that their respective advocates seek to apply to Pizarro. The General, however, disdains 'loyalty' as just another word under which men hide from their baser natures, and with which they seek to camouflage their selfishness and greed.

A minor theme, which assumes central importance in Shaffer's two other major plays (*Five Finger Exercise* and *Equus*) is that of the *torments of adolescence*. This theme occurs here in Young Martin's part in the story, which concerns a development and growth that is as much psychic as physical: the spurs Martin wins goad his mind as much as they mark his achievement.

Style

Although the play is very tightly organized, the enormous amount of material that Shaffer needed and chose to include in it could not be encompassed in a naturalistic drama relying on the presentation of realistic detail and action. The dramatic unities of time and place could have no space in a piece which spans more than four years of history and covers several thousand miles of travelling both by land and sea. The playwright, therefore, deliberately set out to avoid realism and to conjure the effects of jungles and mountains through a combination of stage effects (lighting etc.) and the evocative power of description. In a note on the playing of *The Royal Hunt of the Sun* Shaffer states that, 'As for staging, austerity and non-literalness should be the key-notes.' In a generation when the theatre at large was starved of the spectacular element, he set out 'to realize on stage a kind of "total" theatre involving not only words but rites, mimes, masks and magics'. By means of colourful pageantry, ritualized movement and a haunting range of calls, chanting and stylized patterns of speech, Shaffer achieved, through a combination of austerity and richness, an experience that was entirely and solely theatrical.

The Incas in particular represent, and need to be repre-sented as, a world totally unfamiliar and unexpected to the audience: 'the fantastic apparition of the pre-Columbian world'. Shaffer insisted that the Incas should be played less naturalistically – certainly in a less Western way – than the Spaniards. They should be masked (half masks in gold) to suggest the relentless uniformity imposed upon them by their social structure; and their walk, posture and speech should be highly formalized, emphasizing the immense over-organized ritual of Inca life.

Add to this the musical fantasia – whined and whispered, sung and shouted as background to the movement; and the centrally symbolic shape of the Sun, whose significance is underlined by the twenty-four scenes of the play and which provides both scenic and aesthetic unity to the action – and one can begin to understand why *The Royal Hunt of the Sun* has been called '*the greatest play of our generation*'.

Language

In many ways it is contrary to Shaffer's dramatic intentions to distinguish for special mention the words of the text from the other theatrical elements and devices which contribute to its complex, magical totality. However, in reading or classroom study it is largely through language that we are able to penetrate the thoughts and feelings of the characters, and it is through language that we are carried on the journey through time and space that is the play. Consistent with the piece's overall aesthetic balance between the austere and the elaborate, its language is alternatively harshly prosaic and richly poetic and marks the difference between the blunt practicality of the ordinary soldiers and the colourful sensitivity of Old Martin's recollections. The vivid similes, both beautiful and brutal, that Martin favours to convey the breathtaking splendour and the agonizing pain of the march through the Andes supply an essential link between his experience and our (the audience's) comprehension. The recurrent metaphors underline the many levels on which the play and its ideas operate: 'my head was one vast plain for feats of daring.' (Act 1, Sc. 1, p.126). In addition to the metaphor of exploration, the text expresses the different dimensions of wealth, both spiritual – 'The priceless mercy of heaven' (1,1,p.129) – and material. And gold itself is presented as staggeringly beautiful – Old Martin's description of Cuzco (2,6,p.181); and excessively repulsive, by Pizarro (2,10,p.196).

Other images that contribute significantly to the language of the play are those associated with the violent beauty of nature demonstrated in plant and animal life. Furthermore, the biblical metaphor concerned with sowing/reaping/feeding that De Nizza employs appositely underlines the agricultural basis of Inca society. Besides Old Martin, Francisco Pizarro is the greatest talker in the play, and his words range from the blunt directness of the military commander to the powerful evocations of his past experiences – 'snakes hung over your heads like bell-ropes' (1,1,p.128) and the rhythmically alliterative strength of his impassioned assaults on traditional customs and values – 'dipping flags and ducking heads' (1,5,p.142). Whether poetic or prosaic, the language of all the Spanish contingent is essentially naturalistic and contrasts sharply and intentionally with the clipped formalized style of Incan speech.

Characters

The Officers
Francisco Pizarro

According to some, Francisco Pizarro was deserted by both his parents and left as a foundling at the door of one of the principal churches in the city of Trujillo: it is even said that he would have perished had he not been suckled by a pig. Whatever the truth of his birth, Pizarro's background is one of deprivation and poverty which have bred in him a fierce determination to win for himself those privileges which, because of his illegitimacy, society has denied him. Pizarro feels no affection or patriotic sentiment towards his native Spain for it has given him nothing (1,1,p.131) and in any case the only legacy it has given the world is greed and covetousness (1,6,p.144). He had made himself what he is (the son of his own deeds) by the sweat of his own efforts ('an old slogger') and has become a local and national hero whose success has won him wealth and position. But lacking the breeding, title, inherited honour and the place in society which these would guarantee, his achievements are not enough, and his motives for winning the command of the expedition to Peru are to gain for himself fame and a name that will go down in history.

It is no coincidence that Pizarro is acquainted with the name of Tamburlaine – spelt Tamberlain in the play (2,3,p.169) – for he too had risen from the obscurity of being a shepherd to rule a vast empire; and the more recent sensational success of Cortez, the son of a poor landowner who had left home at sixteen to become the conqueror of the Aztecs, cannot have been far from Pizarro's mind. One of a long tradition of men whose determined ambition has caused them to cast aside traditional authority, Pizarro has no respect for the superficial manifestations of office, as represented by men like Estete. Nor does he trust the loyalties to the Crown, the Church or the Army, which he believes are merely institutions to protect men from facing the truths of their individual function in the world. The crown is revealed to him as hollow and gluttonous; the Church wicked and suspect; and the Army a deluded band of cowards seeking a cause by which to justify its butchery. Pizarro, however, accepts these institutions, exploits and manipulates them as long as they can serve to fulfil his objectives: nevertheless he has a profound disdain for all those allegiances whose strength lies in the deceptive power of the word: 'put down the word Gentleman to blot up the blood' (1,5,p.141) – believing that deeds present the only irrefutable argument.

When we first meet Pizarro he is a tough, experienced professional soldier who has had his youthful idealism and hopes shattered by the harsh and violent life he has led. The causes for which he once fought have lost their attraction; he has become disillusioned by an awareness of the inevitable cruelty of the cycle of nature; and the attempt to liberate himself from the entanglements of his birth has left him without joy. He appears, therefore, as a sardonic pragmatist, a melancholic realist intensely conscious of the futility of existence, living his life between two hates (1,5,p.142). Stripped of any kind of conventional faith, his soul frostbitten and his heart hardened, he is set on proving that he can meet any challenge and overcome any obstacle. However, one impediment that he feels he has no way of avoiding is time: he is haunted by the bitter realization of the constraint it imposes on man's freedom and is further frustrated by the depressing inevitability of death. Though a man who has tried everything, thought about everything, been disgusted or disenchanted by everything, he has never ceased from searching for something to believe in, something by which he can cheat time, find strength and stability and overcome the only ultimate reality – death.

Shaffer's play, therefore, traces not only the conquest and discovery of Peru but also the spiritual and mental development of one of the world's great explorers. In the mysterious silence of the Andes, Pizarro, the Catholic atheist, explores what and who he is and, though he does not find the answers he has expected, he does recover a little of his taste for life. Thousands of miles from the commands of his King and the decrees of his Pope – and himself a general whose authority is unquestioned and jealously guarded – the illiterate upstart becomes the soaring over-reacher. And by exploiting the mistaken illusion in his deity he finds himself in the position of being giver and taker of life for one whose claim to be a god is undisputed by his people. It is a curious fate that brings him – nominally in search of gold, fame and a place in history – to the land of Atahuallpa; for the Sun God might be something he can believe in, a being who by definition not only represents the possibility of escaping from time but also of cheating death. Atahuallpa has Pizarro enthralled by his own conviction that he cannot die, that he rules death and that, at the reappearance of his father the Sun, he too will rise again. Not only does the inescapable logic of the Sun's immortality seem to provide Pizarro with the solution to one of life's insoluble riddles but, paradoxically, Pizarro himself becomes something that the Inca can for a while put his faith in – the white god from the east who will inaugurate a new era. Both, however, are ultimately cheated. Atahuallpa, because the Spaniard's deceitfulness exposes him for the treacherous opportunist he is: one for whom expediency outweighs principle and policy overrides justice. And Pizarro is disillusioned because the Inca does not rise again, his empire falls in ruins; and soon afterwards the General, who himself unwillingly and incredulously brought this about, falls too. However, the mental and spiritual conflict that consumes Pizarro when he realizes that he must kill one who is a mirror image of himself, one who has given him complete trust, is the core of the drama and the source of a faint hope. For once, as a man, Pizarro holds on – out of a deep 'useless', barely acknowledged affection – to the life-thread of another man. He celebrates in his stubbornness the wonder of life: he is left with no answer, ultimately with no existence. But, in a paradoxical sense, by finding real grief he recovers joy.

Hernando de Soto

Pizarro's second-in-command contrasts sharply with his superior in background, conduct and attitude to life. He is one of the Spanish aristocracy, a Knight, who has inherited a recognized position in society and accepted the traditional values and beliefs that go with it. His assured confidence in the validity of the contemporary view of the world is under-lined by his dramatically ironic acceptance of the Ptolemaic theory of the universe upon which it was founded (1,10,p.156). In addition to the rank and title to which he has succeeded, de Soto has inherited a strict code of conduct and a sense of honour which make him a staunch patriot and a resolute supporter of his monarch, in whose cause he joins Pizarro's expedition. He is also a confirmed member of the Catholic Church and is quite prepared to die for Spain and Christ in the service of his God and King. Having chosen his ideals he pursues them with unwavering conviction, showing no conscience over the necessity of killing in the name of Christ (2,1,p.164), and displaying little concern for the moral dilemma over the right of conquest. To this extent he is a pragmatist who accepts the realities of war and whose faith in the cause for which he is fighting provides him with the justification to prepare the way for the coming of Christ.

De Soto is an experienced campaigner and capable leader and it is no surprise that Pizarro delegates to him the reconnaissance expedition that leads him to discover the riches of Cuzco (2,6,p.181). Despite his superior upbringing, de Soto has total respect for his general's superior rank and – though he does not totally understand what Pizarro hopes to find in Peru – does all he can to help lighten his commander's responsibilities and worries (2,8,p.190). De Soto is a shrewd tactician who is calmly efficient in moments of crisis while being sensitive to the necessity of maintaining the morale of his men. However, when the discipline of the force is threatened by covetousness he is quick to enforce order, and his strict sense of justice ensures that Rodas receives no reward for his cowardice (2,8,p.190). Despite his firmness, however, the Cavalier has a 'tender' side to his character: his cultured breeding is displayed in his capacity to appreciate the aesthetic beauty of the golden objects that comprise Atahuallpa's ransom; whereas Pizarro, like everyone else, recognizes only their value as payment.

Fundamentally, though, de Soto is a man of his word and it is in this respect that he contributes significantly to the play's central conflict. He clearly foresees the danger of Pizarro's entering an agreement whose terms he will be unable to honour, and adheres to his belief that principles cannot be altered by policy (2,3,p.169). So convinced is he of this fundamental truth that he is prepared to take his chances against the overwhelming numbers of the Incan army rather than recommend the expedient removal of a man who has been deceived by insincerity. For where man cannot be trusted to keep his word and honour his oath, social, political and spiritual chaos must ensue; and, as an essential representative of order in the play, this is something that de Soto will never condone.

Miguel Estete

Estete is the Royal Veedor or delegate on the expedition and is intensely aware of his role and function. In Panama he attempts to place himself in a position of supreme authority above Pizarro and infuriates the general with his disparaging reminder of the duty owed to God and the King. As Charles I's representative he considers it his right to receive the ambassador of the Inca (1,6,p.145), though his haughty manner seems likely to provoke open conflict long before Pizarro is ready to challenge his adversaries. He is contemptuous of the native Inca peoples (1,4,p.137), showing no awareness of injustice in directing the iron of Spain against the feathers of Peru, and approving their rigorous conversion. He despises Pizarro's lack of breeding and feels it as a personal insult that the King has awarded the command of the expedition to a dangerous madman. Even though he accepts Pizarro's military authority, the threat that he poses to the General's supremacy causes him to be left in charge of the Spanish rearguard garrison, and he takes no part in the action from Act 1, Scene 5 to Act 2, Scene 8.

His fanatical patriotism and zealous sense of duty towards the crown leads Estete to eschew all motive of self-interest and personal ambition (1,5,p.140). He regards as a form of blasphemy any insult to the King's name and is eager to secure the royal fifth portion of Atahuallpa's ransom. Yet below the superficial display of virtuousness and moral rectitude lies an uncompromising Machiavellian cunning, which is prepared to recommend any means to justify the end. Even though he fails to persuade de Candia to assassinate the Inca, hoping thus to absolve King Charles of moral implication, he is not above tempting Pizarro to adopt a tyrranic role in order to achieve his purpose (2,10,p.195). However, when subtle argument and deviousness have failed, it is Estete, astutely sensing the mood of the majority of the Spanish camp, who leads the revolt that forces Pizarro's hand.

de Candia

De Candia is not a Spaniard and therefore, significantly, he lacks all those loyalties – to King, country and a common bond of companionship – which on the surface unite the other officers and soldiers. Furthermore, he recognizes no spiritual allegiance to the Catholic church or its crusading cause, as his sarcastic rejection of de Nizza's offer of confession, before the slaughter at Cajamarca, goes to prove; he is sharply aware of the contradictory nature of the priest's mission (1,9,p.153). Living up to his reputation as a Venetian, he is shamelessly self-interested, a professional opportunist who relies on no principle to govern his action except expediency and performs his deadly task with cynical efficiency. As commander of the artillery, he is in charge of the invaders' most powerful and terrifying weapon, which deploys without conscience against an enemy bearing axes and spears. He has joined Pizarro for purely material motives and is thoroughly sceptical of the bogus sense of honour and duty that, he believes, conceals the fundamental meanness and ruthlessness of the Spanish cause (2,8,p.190). De Candia is unpityingly pragmatic and quickly assesses what needs to be done: he is not slow to support Estete's coup.

Diego de Trujillo

As Master of Horse, Diego is entrusted with a resource which, because the horse was unknown to the Incas, proved to be a key weapon of terror in the conquest of central and southern America. As a conscript, he is an officer of low rank who is not consulted on important decisions and is respectfully obedient to his superiors. He has the closest contact with the ordinary soldiers, though the authority he holds over them has to be reinforced with violence when the men are on the point of mutiny. His most important dramatic function lies in the appeal he makes to Pizarro's sense of comradeship and of loyalty to his men, though his admiration only goes to prove to the old general the hollow virtue of 'Gang-love' (2,10,p.197).

The Men
Old Martin

Old Martin's primary function in the play is as a narrator who is able to coordinate a chronicle of events that covers a period of four years and many thousands of miles of journeying. He introduces the main characters (Act 1, Scenes 1 and 2) and locates the various scenes, both geographically and, where essential to an understanding of the time-scale, historically. Old Martin, therefore, provides us with all the necessary information which is not supplied by the play's action and thus is an agent of dramatic economy enabling the author to focus entirely on the key moments of human conflict. Perhaps the most notable example of this function comes right at the end of the play where Atahuallpa's trial (a traditional source of dramatic material for playwrights) is dealt with in little more than two sentences. As a narrator, Old Martin also helps us to bridge the imaginary gaps that neither factual information nor stage scenery could be expected to fill. Like a Shakespearean Chorus, his vividly evocative descriptions enable us to identify with the experiences he is recalling and his verbal portrait of the Andes and the suffering of the Spanish contingent crossing them (1,6;1,7–8,pp.143;149–51), is especially powerful.

As the last surviving member of Pizarro's force, Old Martin's position as an eye-witness is particularly important, since he is able to supply evidence of events we might otherwise be tempted to dismiss as exaggerations or impossibilities, and he can thus convince us of their truth and reality.

Distanced from the occurrences by more than two generations, Ruiz is able to adopt the role of chronicler who is responsible for the view of history presented in the play: 'I've done for you' (2,12,p.204). And he encourages the audience to see events through his eyes. The historical perspective enables him to be as objective as possible despite having lived the experiences he describes; and though his final words are tinged with obvious sadness and regret, he is no moralist, but leaves his listeners to form their own judgements.

Seen from Old Martin's point of view, the play is an auto-biography that traces the sudden shattering of the innocent idealism of youth in the Square of Cajamarca to the joyless disillusionment of age. The submissive colonialist of the end of the play, his faith in human nature undermined, has been reduced to a state of mind similar to that of his hero general at the play's outset, where experience has deadened any prospect of hope.

Young Martin

Young Martin Ruiz not only figures in the play as the youthful former self of its narrator, but by means of this ingenious dramatic device reminds us of the adolescent dreams Pizarro once possessed. (1,1,p.130). A significant point of detail pro-vides Martin and his general with the same birthplace, thus not only reinforcing the similarities between the two men in old age but emphasizing the inevitable cycle of hope and despair, which is part of life. When we first encounter Martin, he is a sensitive young man whose view of the world has been formed by what he has read in books: he is a romantic dreamer with a quixotic view of reality. He is a staunch patriot and has an implicit belief in the traditional codes of chivalry, which are based on honour, trust, service, courage and the glory of fight-ing for a noble cause; his faith in these principles is unshakeable even in the face of harsh cynicism (1,5,p.142). When Pizarro, the local hero, walks into his life, the hope of realizing his dreams materializes, and the journey upon which he sets out with the general to discover Peru is one in which he also discovers him-self and the realities of material existence. The theories that have formed the basis of Martin's adolescent hopes suffer a severe re-examination in the unfamiliar mountains of South America.

Even after his sudden and violent initiation into the real, adult world on the day in which he wins his spurs and loses his innocence, the 'little lord of hope' is not totally disillusioned even though he initially professes to prefer a noble death rather than a life that shames the name of Christ.

Although disenchanted with the barbarous crusading spirit of the expedition, Young Martin still continues to worship his general and serve him with a loyalty that touches even the hard-hearted old warrior. However, when Martin's hero breaks his word with one whom he has come to respect and almost love, the foundations of the young man's conviction crumble and he forgets all codes of conduct and restraint in his final impassioned appeal for the values he has upheld.

Young Martin's literacy is an important dimension of the play since, in the first place, it substantiates his elder's function as a historian. However, his education and ability to learn quickly also make him an invaluable ally to Pizarro in his strange relationship with Atahuallpa and in the incident with Felipillo (2,2,p.166). In a series of events that are determined by the importance of 'the word' – keeping and breaking an oath, the word of God – Martin's unique command of language gives him a profound power, which Atahuallpa shrewdly recognizes (2,7,p.185), but which proves to be totally ineffectual against fanaticism and greed.

The soldiers

The conscripts that Pizarro enlists in his home town of Trujillo are all very similar in background but different enough as individuals to make them interesting characters. They are coarse illiterate peasants who have little attachment to the land of their birth and nothing to lose by leaving it. Having lived a life of tedious poverty, their sole motive for joining the expedition is the prospect of gold, though the common purpose that binds them in a fragile comradeship quickly breaks down under the threat of danger and in the face of selfish greed.

Vasca

He is shrewd and calculating and makes no secret of his craving for wealth and power. He has no love or respect for his country and his black humour suggests that he has few feelings for people, either. In Cajamarca he turns out to be a danger-ous anarchist who attempts to lead a rebellion in which law-lessness and greed prevail.

Rodas

The tailor is a blunt sceptic who is unmoved by the prospect of adventure and wealth and is not the most willing of Pizarro's conscripts. A loud-mouthed coward who does not recognize the spirit of comradeship, he remains with Estete's garrison while the others risk their lives at Cajamarca and displays his vindictiveness when he receives no reward for his faint-heartedness.

Domingo

The cooper is probably the most simple-minded of all the common soldiers. He has a superstitious belief in omens and a blind faith which causes him to see his survival in Cajamarca as a miracle. The depressing state of his trade has been a prime motive for leaving Spain, but he has no wish to be supper for an American cannibal.

Salinas

The smith is a coarse warm hearted man whose attraction to the prospect of gold does not destroy his sense of fellowship.

The priests

Vincente de Valverde

As chaplain to the expedition, Valverde obviously has little doubt that the right of conquest carries with it the right to convert. A peasant at heart, he is ruthlessly zealous and might be expected to have supported those ecclesiastical authorities of the time who quoted Joshua's defeat of Jericho as a precedent for righteous extermination of infidels, even though the heathen Americans had been living in peaceful isolation and in no way violating or harassing Christian territory. His Christianity is based on a rather primitive, unquestioning view of God which sees all unbelievers as the legitimate prey of his faithful warriors and the declared victims of his followers' wrath and vengeance. As a member of the Dominican order, he can be associated with that religious fanaticism which gave birth and justification to the Inquisition and the rigorous enthusiasm with which he promotes the conversion of the Incas strongly emphasizes the unpitying nature of his methods. He believes that Atahuallpa is the Anti-Christ, an agent of the devil; and this is only too strongly reinforced when the Inca suggests that his people are dispensable in the cause of protecting and preserving their god-sovereign (2,4,p.175).

At the beginning of the play (1,1,p.129), Valverde's hollow appeal to the missionary spirit of the villagers is combined with a form of religious bribery, in which his offer of absolution only goes to illustrate the fact that he is prepared to employ any methods or arguments to achieve his aims. Furthermore, his application of biblical metaphor – especially the fundamentally significant contrast between material and spiritual riches – shows that he has achieved only a very superficial, simplistic interpretation of biblical teaching. The result is that he is unable to engage in the complexities of theological debate and is no match for Atahuallpa's sharp exposure of doctrinal paradox (2,4,p.173). He has a strong sense of the awe and respect due to his order and his own position as

Christ's spokesman: during the fruitless debate of Act 2, Scene 10 Pizarro accuses him of playing at God. Valverde is a dangerous man when he feels that either the name of God or his own authority has suffered challenge or insult. It is in such circumstances (at the end of each Act of the play) that he issues a frenzied appeal for God to strike the Inca heretics – and his sense of legal rectitude seems perfectly satisfied by the ludicrously impracticable and unjust requirement that he is responsible for delivering.

We should not, however, look upon Valverde as a dramatic caricature whose primary function is to demonstrate the neurotic hypocrisy of the Church and its representatives. He, and many priests like him blinded by religious ardour and a paranoid fear of the Apocalypse, must have seemed only too real to the unfortunate American Indians.

de Nizza

As a representative of the Franciscan order, with its traditions of compassion and gentleness, Marcos de Nizza provides a clear and intentional contrast with his colleague at the beginning of the play. While Valverde is fervently blessing the agents of divine retribution, de Nizza envisages the positive benefits of conquest, which will be based on the virtues of mercy, pity and love. As opposed to the Dominican's rather clumsy handling of doctrinal concepts, the Franciscan applies with dexterity the remarkable notion that the Christian explorers will bring the spiritual food of their religion to the starving unconverted natives. His God is a New Testament God, whose strength lies not in the terror invoked by the threat of punishment but in his ability to provide a liberation of the spirit manifested in the free expression of love. De Nizza is initially impressed by the beauty of the Quechua language and the contentedness of the Inca people, and supports Pizarro's plan at Cajamarca on the grounds that 'it would avoid bloodshed'.

However, once Atahuallpa has been captured and the priests
have been able to find out about the Inca religion and the
society which supports it, de Nizza's attitude changes to
condemn as a living hell the land which he once thought of as a
paradise. The main reason for this transition lies in his conviction that the freedom of the individual spirit is deliberately
suppressed by the rulers of Peru so that there can be no spontaneous expression of love or even awareness of real happiness
since unhappiness is unknown. Such conditions are in fundamental opposition to the Christian concept of Sin and the
moral virtues that man must pursue in order to overcome it
which alone can offer hope of salvation. Despite the intellec-
tual foundation that supports his faith, the more Atahuallpa
doggedly maintains his belief in his own deity and immortality,
the more de Nizza realizes the futility of attempting to explain
the basic precepts of Christianity to him and becomes convinced that to save love in the world you must kill lovelessness
(2,10,p.196). At the end of the play, therefore, de Nizza is just
as convinced as his colleague that the evil represented by
Atahuallpa cannot be spared, but must be exorcized and
rooted out though he can, presumably, find some consolation
in being able to baptize the Inca before his execution.

The Indians
Atahuallpa

The sovereign emperor of Peru is not only an immensely
powerful personality in his own right but also a symbol of the
mysterious civilization that Pizarro and his Spaniards set out
to conquer. As a dramatic figure he is the source of that spectacle and magical excitement which Shaffer designed to capture and the elaborate finery and colour that accompany his
appearance strongly contrast with the sordid disarray of his
conquerors. To the Incas he is untouchable and invested with
an awesome purity which demands supreme reverence and

respect, all of which are underlined by the utter simplicity of the white robes in which he greets Pizarro at Cajamarca. But long before this stunning revelation, the power of his presence has been sensed by the Spanish soldiers. Even in captivity he maintains an air of dignified majesty and remains an object of profound veneration: the highly sophisticated rituals of everyday life are not denied him and the completeness of his authority is demonstrated to every Spaniard who attempts to supersede his command (see 2,4,pp.172–6). It is this very autocracy, however, that both initially preserves and ultimately condemns him. For while the Spaniards have in their control an absolute ruler whose authority is unchallenged his value to them as a hostage is inestimable: however, as soon as he becomes a political and military liability the danger that he threatens far outweighs his personal worth.

As a member of the Inca royal family, Atahuallpa has an implicit faith in his divine origin and mission and conducts himself – even in death – with assurance and self-confidence (2,11,p,198). Even though he is prepared to accept he may have lost political power, he remains convinced of his spiritual superiority to the Christian traitors with whom his fate rests and suffers no doubt or inner conflict of faith. However, it is his severe arrogance at the beginning of the play which fatally restrains him from ordering the annihilation of Pizarro's pathetic force of invaders and his refusal to listen to his generals' cautious warnings and his high-priest's fatal omens directly derive from a fundamental conviction in his own infallibility. Even so his resolute persuasion that Pizarro is the mystical White God who is returning to bless him (1,7,p.148) may suggest an underlying desire to have the political power that he has recently seized from Huascar ratified by divine favour. Atahuallpa is initially deluded by Pizarro's apparent ability to make the Inca people praise a Christian God though the hollowness of their words is soon confirmed by the general's lying betrayal.

The Spanish chroniclers described the Inca as 'a man of good appearance and manner, although somewhat thick-set. He had a large face, handsome and fierce, his eyes reddened with blood. He spoke with much gravity as a great ruler. He made very lively arguments: when the Spaniards understood them they realized that he was a wise man. He was a cheerful man, although unsubtle. When he spoke to his own people he was incisive and showed no pleasure.' Despite the trap that he allows himself to be drawn into and the fact that he is duped for a second time by Pizarro's deceitfulness, Atahuallpa is clearly a shrewd and clever man. Not only is he quick to see the possibility of buying his liberty but his perceptive exposure of the contradictions within some aspects of Christian doctrine reveals an intelligence far superior to that of most of his captors. Even though he is illiterate, he quickly comprehends the power of written symbols whose influence over the minds as well as the bodies of men is tragically demonstrated by the vengeful disciples whose victim he ultimately becomes.

Atahuallpa is also an intuitive judge of character and his sensitive assessment of Pizarro's political motives and personal beliefs (or lack of them) demonstrates an inherent wisdom. Despite de Nizza's condemnation of his totalitarian rule and accusation of lovelessness, Atahuallpa does show a sense of responsibility for his people and laments the suffering he foresees for them (2,3,p.168). However, where his own safety is endangered not only his people but even his priests and generals are dispensible (2,4,p.175). Indeed, below the natural grace and dignity their lies a simmering violence which is revealed in his ruthless desire for revenge (2,7,p.186) on Pizarro's butchers and his outraged fury against de Nizza's insult to his self-conception (2,4,p.174).

Atahuallpa's intense, involved and, in some ways, obscure relationship with Pizarro is based to a large extent on his recognition of the similarities which unite himself to the Spaniard. Not only are they both illegitimate, both illiterate and, in their own ways, usurpers of power but both are un-scrupulous men of action. However, whereas Atahuallpa represents for Pizarro a form of spiritual hope through which he may overcome the inevitability of death, the Inca – from his supreme position of unique omnipotence – rejects the melan-cholic view of the world presented to him by the priests. Like Christ, who was martyred at the same age because of the threat he was thought to represent, Atahuallpa is able to bring peace and comfort to the man he knows will be his assassin. However, despite the parallel, which becomes obvious to Pizarro (2,11,p.199), Atahuallpa's faith in his own resurrection proves to be an arrogant illusion, and his death marks the end of his dynasty and empire.

Villac Umu

The high priest of the Temple of the Sun at Cuzco held his post for life, was married and held an authority which was little less than that of the Inca. He was of noble lineage and had power over all shrines and temples to which he appointed and removed priests. He was believed to have the ability to communicate with the supernatural powers and predict the course of future events through divination. Villac Umu is a key part of the ritualized ceremony which accompanies the Inca and in the first part his ominous warnings – 'Ware! Ware!' – become a kind of liturgical chant. When he meets the Christian missionaries he is unable to comprehend the spiritual basis of their concept of God and is largely responsible in the second Act for proclaiming the orthodox doctrine of Inca religion (2,4,p.172).

Challcuchima

Challcuchima was one of the three important generals who supported Atahuallpa in the civil war of succession against his brother Huascar. History indicates that Challcuchima was not the commander of the army that Atahuallpa had with him at Cajamarca when Pizarro arrived, but was rather holding the area around Jauja (about half way between Cajamarca and Cuzco) against the possibility of a further rising by Huascar's supporters. It was only as a result of Hernando Pizarro's expedition to Pachacamac in March 1533 that he was persuaded to join his emperor, thus giving the Spaniards power over one of the most powerful military men in Peru as well as its ruler. By placing Challcuchima with Atahuallpa from the beginning of the play, Shaffer not only achieves dramatic economy but provides the Inca with an adviser whose shrewd common sense becomes all too evident as events progress. His main dramatic function is to issue the daring challenge that provokes Pizarro to scale the mountain road to Cajamarca. Once Atahuallpa is in the hands of the Spaniards, Challcuchima is as impotent as his emperor.

Felipillo

An Indian boy employed by Pizarro as an interpreter, he is also used as the evidence which tempts the ordinary Spaniards to join Pizarro's army. He has obviously become a Christian convert, but once back in South America his dishonesty and deceitfulness, his impudence and lust suggest how the innocence of many natives in the future will be perverted by greed and selfishness. As such he represents a profoundly ironic dramatic comment on the moral justification of crusading conquest.

Other Indians

All the other Indians who appear in the play, including the Chieftain and Headsman and the two women who accompany the Inca, serve to emphasize – either by word or deed – the supreme authority of Atahuallpa. They are totally subservient and show a reverential awe which is powerfully demonstrated by their prostration in his presence and their blind self-sacrifice on his behalf in the great massacre at Cajamarca. While

Atahuallpa is held captive by the Spaniards, the Indians continue to respect the Inca's omnipotence, and no attempt to rescue him is made without the command which the Emperor's bond with Pizarro prevents him from giving. Brought up to recognize an unquestioning obedience:

Ten generations, ten million Indians had heard it said: 'The Inca knows all. The Inca cannot be mistaken. The Inca is immortal.' But suddenly the monotonous voice was stilled. The Inca was dead. What could they do when they only knew how to obey? Ten million slaves held out their wrists for Spanish chains. Jean Descola

Act 1, The Hunt. Scene summaries, textual notes and revision questions

Scene 1 Trujillo, Spain, June 1529 (pp.125–32)

Old Martin introduces himself as the narrator of an amazing story in which he became involved as a boy burning with patriotic dreams of glory. He recalls the day he encountered Francisco Pizarro, the famous Spanish explorer, recruiting in his home town for a new expedition to Peru. Despite the scepticism of Rodas, the tailor, Pizarro attracts several men with the gold displayed by an Indian slave and the evangelical spirit added by his chaplain, Valverde. Young Martin Ruiz is overjoyed to be engaged as a page. Finally, Pizarro explains to his second-in-command, de Soto, that he is returning to the Pacific not for fortune, but eternal fame.

Crucifixes, sharpened to resemble swords An important visual symbol which, by combining an image of Christ on the cross (the crucifix) and the features of a sword, reminds us that the early Spanish explorers were crusaders as well as conquerors.

hidalgo One of the lower Spanish nobility: a gentleman by birth.

Save you all Short for 'God save you all': a conventional greeting.

Peru In 1522 Pascual de Andagoya sailed along the coast of modern Colombia in an attempt to make contact with a tribe called 'Viru' or 'Biru': the name of this tribe, altered to 'Peru' came to be applied to unknown lands lying to the south.

counting House Renaissance term for a commercial bank.

conquered The title commonly adopted by the Spanish explorers, conquistador, meant 'conqueror'.

vault A tomb: an unsavoury image through which Old Martin seems to be recalling the bloodshed and killing that the Spaniards had inflicted upon Peru.

wits turn easier One can go mad more quickly.

Indians When Columbus began his original voyage of exploration he was hoping to discover a sea route to India. Despite his unintentional discovery of the Americas, the native people of these unexplored territories were described as 'Indians'.

The inside of my head was one vast plain for feats of daring This powerful metaphor indicates the force of Martin's imagination and his dreams of heroic adventure.

Don Cristobal A medieval authority on the codes of chivalry whose book contained the articles of Martin's juvenile beliefs (his Bible).

two expeditions to the New World See notes on the historical background to the play. Pizarro had served in expeditions to the central Americas in 1513 and 1524.

at over sixty years Authority differs over the date of Pizarro's birth. John Hemming supports 1478, Prescott is uncertain – probably it was not far from 1471; but Shaffer's reference would place it earlier than 1469, since the first scene takes place in 1529.

the King Charles I (1500–58, King of Spain 1516–56); Holy Roman Emperor Charles V (1519–56); the last emperor to try to realize the medieval ideal of a unified empire embracing the entire Christian world. He retired to a monastery in 1556.

Viceroy A vice-king, acting in the name and by the authority of the supreme ruler.

Trujillo A small town below the Sierra de Guadalupe in the province of Estremadura in west-central Spain.

resting here – Rest Rodas probably means simply 'staying here'. Pizarro seems to indulge in a little word play: his curt 'rest' suggesting that Rodas lacks the energy and courage needed for an overseas campaign.

Seventeen Old Martin's lie emphasizes his desire, when adolescent, to be grown up in order to qualify for military service.

old slogger One who has achieved everything by sweat and labour: Pizarro has never known the privileges of inherited position.

mercenary a professional paid soldier, one not fighting for a cause.

a closed book Pizarro knows nothing of the theoretical codes of combat: his soldiercraft is based on practical experience.

all books are closed to me Pizarro was illiterate and is making a wry joke at his own expense here.

my Lord Martin's words of address indicate an adoration that is almost profane.

alter the heathen The early explorers of the Americas had a spiritual as well as a material goal. The right of conquest carried with it the right to convert, and thus heathen lands became the legitimate prey of the Spanish missionaries.

Cavalier The Spanish word for 'Knight': a titled nobleman.

Cordoba Francisco Hernandez Cordoba (1475–1526): Spanish soldier and explorer who campaigned in Panama with Pedrarias in 1514 and undertook the exploration of Nicaragua in 1524. Beheaded by Pedrarias in 1526 for his defection to Cortez, the conqueror of the Aztecs.

llama A small woolly animal of the camel family, sacred to the Incas. At the Festival of the Sun they were sacrificed as burnt offerings, and their flesh eaten sacramentally at a banquet by the Lord of the Incas and his nobles, then distributed to the rest of the community with sacred maize cakes.

Balboa See *Historical background*. Pizarro was an officer in Balboa's force which discovered the Pacific ocean in 1513.

aloe A plant known for its bitter juice. The leaves of the larger American variety were often used by primitive tribes as a kind of paper.

swamps. A forest like the beard of the world Pizarro is probably recalling his painful route through the jungles of Panama to the Pacific.

men that eat each other The natives of central America, especially the Aztecs, had a tradition of human sacrifice and religious cannibalism.

I took only two steps Pizarro's first contact with the Inca civilization was at Tumbez on the narrow coastal strip of northern Peru.

Ecuador See map. A large part of the country was included in the Inca empire.

Down Kneel down.

condemned to eternal flame A primitive Christian philosophy that consigned all non-believers to hell.

lift Steal.

The priceless mercy of heaven Valverde tries to justify the material objectives of conquest by suggesting that the natives will receive in return a spiritual wealth that cannot be valued in material terms. A specious argument.

absolve Acquit, purify. Valverde is indulging in religious bribery here.

hissing A substituted obscenity!

that'll be your slave The native Indian, like Felipillo

employment for a dog Work that distinguishes humans only a little from animals.

Toledo An important provincial city south of Madrid where on 26 July 1529 the Spanish Queen signed a *Capitulaciòn* (authorization) for Pizarro to explore Peru.

yourself, just as you were Young Martin reminds Pizarro of his own days of youthful innocence and optimism.

Dreamers deserve what they get i.e. disillusioned by the harsh truths of reality.

lodestone A metal ore with magnetic properties; the meaning here must be 'force of attraction'.

Gold turns into metal Gold is reduced to its basic properties, an element of no intrinsic value.

infirmity Pizarro bears the pains of an old wound. See p.134.

my father couldn't own to my mother Pizarro was an illegitimate child: the relationship between his father and mother could not therefore be legally 'acknowledged'.

arquebus A portable type of field gun usually supported by a tripod when in operation.

Balboa's See note, p.48.

the world said 'No' The world rejected him. Pizarro resents the fact that because he was a bastard, he could not be recognized by society.

A name A reputation and recognition denied to him by his obscure origins.

You inherited your honour De Soto's noble background and attitudes contrast sharply with those of his commander.

Scene 2 Panama, Central America, December 1530 (pp.133–5)

Having reached the Spanish base at Panama, Old Martin recalls the blessing of the expedition and introduces its members. Estete's arrogance incites Pizarro to demonstrate his authority while at the same time revealing what he has suffered as a soldier. The General explains with blunt frankness his view of the military life he has led and scorns his page's noble values and beliefs.

polyphony The harmony of several individual melodies.

St John the Evangelist 27 December.

consecrated Sanctified.

muster Official list of officers and men.

one hundred and eighty-seven There is some disagreement about the exact size of the force in the various accounts. The difference between the number (167) quoted in Old Martin's opening speech and the 187 mentioned here can be explained by the fact that the force was reduced at a later stage by the 20-man garrison left with Estete (see also 1,6,p.146).

bringers of food de Nizza's whole speech operates by means of a metaphor based on the symbolic meaning of Christian communion. The explorers will thus bring the spiritual food of their religion to the starving unconverted natives of South America.

sow their fields The corn seeds which provide the substance of physical existence will be replaced by spiritual seeds which will grow to sustain a much deeper existence.

we are their New World An inspired idea, which reverses the traditional view of the conquest. The Christians, while entering a new world in geographical terms, will themselves bring a new world of religious experience to unilluminated natives.

Almagro Diego de Almagro entered a partnership with Pizarro and Hernando de Luque in 1524 to explore Colombia and Ecuador.

tumbled Motley, varied in character.

ginger Keen, positively motivated.

Veedor Deputy: the word also meant 'spy' in Spanish.

before and after Order of rank; social or political hierarchy.

You watch me Young Martin is keen to show that he is no coward.

Dungballs Rubbish: an emphatic obscenity!

So they build ... bigness Men construct social systems to protect themselves against the awareness of their individual insignificance and vulnerability.

Court, Army, Church Political, military and religious institutions.

colt A young, untamed (unbroken) horse.

break for its sightless track Tame for its infinite path. the phrase is based on the conventional metaphor of the 'road of life' whose end cannot be seen.

a yard of ungrowable children A courtyard of people with minds that will never develop, because they refuse to accept the truths of reality.

blue dead The body becomes blue as the blood cools.

green dead The flesh becomes green as it decays. Both phrases could, however, refer to the different coloured uniforms worn by the dead soldiers.

nightmare game ... reason A horrifying game through which men try to justify their animal (brutal) behaviour.

hacking off limbs Pizarro deliberately employs stark words to emphasize to Martin the cruelty of battle.

wild cats Pizarro may have in mind here the Jaguar, which the Incas, out of fear for the animal, regularly tried to placate with sacred offerings.

awe Reverential fear: Pizarro means that wild animals do not respect any code of chivalry.

Scene 3 The northern province of the Inca empire,
Spring 1532 (pp.135–6)

News is brought to the Emperor Atahuallpa that strange
men on strange animals have been sighted in the northern
province of his empire. Atahuallpa recalls the ancient Inca
legend of a returning white god; while his general Challcuchima advises caution, and his high priest Villac Umu warns
of recent unfavourable omens.

Inca Emperor: a title also applied to the royal family and
  subsequently to the tribe that it headed.
huge golden sun Inti, the sun god whose physical embodiment
  the Emperor (Inca) was thought to be, was usually represented
  in holy places by a human face on a ray-splayed disc.
terracotta Reddish brown, i.e. the colour of terracotta (baked
  earth) ware. The standard dress of the Peruvians was a large
  rectangular cloak of brown wool, knotted across the chest or on
  one shoulder.
Chasqui Courier or messenger.
Farthest Province The northern province around Quito.
  Pizarro had spent most of 1531 exploring the coast of Ecuador
  before reaching Tumbez in early 1532.
sheep The Peruvian natives did not know of horses: they could
  only explain Pizarro's cavalry in terms of those animals with
  which they were acquainted.
White God According to ancient legend Viracocha, the creator
  god of the Incas, and pre-Inca peoples, journeyed widely during
  his lifetime until he came to the shores of Manta (Ecuador)
  where he set off into the Pacific – either by walking on the water
  or in a boat made of his cloak. A sequel to the myth indicated
  that he would one day return in white to judge the Inca peoples.
take the Crown Atahuallpa was a usurper and had ousted his
  legitimate brother in the recent civil war (see introductory
  notes).
Temple in Cuzco The temple of the Sun at Cuzco, the richest
  and most important of all the Inca shrines.
Capac Sovereign.

When the world ... claws The high priest here sees the end of the world in terms of the destruction of natural order so important to stability in the Inca empire. The idea is reminiscent of Shakespeare (cf. *Macbeth* II,4,12–13) and envisages the highest order of birds (eagles, hawks) overthrown by the lower. Villac Umu's words also anticipate the overthrow of the god Atahuallpa by the 'pig-man' Pizarro.

Scene 4 Tumbez, May 1532 (pp.137–9)

At Tumbez, Pizarro's men capture the chief of a local tribe, who provides information about Atahuallpa's victory in the recent civil war. Pizarro is astonished to learn of the Incas' living god, while Valverde is horrified and proceeds upon a rigorous course of conversion. While Pizarro prepares to confront his unseen adversary, Atahuallpa lays plans for a meeting at Cajamarca – despite the continuing fears of his advisers.

Tumbes (Tumbez) The city that had given the Spaniards their first sight of the Inca empire. The civil war had left it in ruins for Pizarro's return in 1532.

the Indians fall silent and passive The importance of the natives' behaviour here cannot be over-estimated for, to a large extent, it explains why Pizarro was able to conquer Peru with such a small force. The Indians were taught one fundamental thing – to obey their leaders and unquestioning obedience was the cement that stabilized their highly stratified society. Leaderless they were impotent.

brownie Dark skinned. The contrast of colour to a large extent explains why Pizarro was thought to be the legendary white god.

God's wounds A common sixteenth century oath; regularly found in Shakespeare abbreviated to 'Zounds'.

Put up Sheathe your sword.

Huascar Atahuallpa's legitimate brother.

one by a not-wife The Quechua (Inca) language lacked a separate word for 'mistress' to indicate that Atahuallpa was illegitimate.

killed his brother The exact sequence of events is
uncertain. Some authorities suggest that Huascar was still alive
at this point and confronting another of Atahuallpa's generals,
Quisquis, outside Cuzco. Shaffer has probably simplified the
situation to heighten the dramatic impact and significance of
Atahuallpa's unchallenged and supreme power.

Son of the Sun Inti, the Sun God, was considered to be the
Emperor's divine ancestor.

He needs no wedded mother Being Europeans, most
chroniclers were concerned to discover which of the two brothers
had the most legitimate claim to the throne. The Incas,
however, did not stress the eldest son's right of succession, being
concerned only that the new Inca should be of royal blood and
fit to rule.

Sapa Inca! Inca Capac Unique god! sovereign lord.

Anti-Christ The title of a great personal opponent of Christ and
his kingdom – expected, in medieval times, to appear before the
end of the world.

shift Change the character of; convert.

rigour Harshness: strict enforcement of the Christian doctrine.

gentle Idolatry The slothful worship of images.

dust This important word in the biblical vocabulary could be
interpreted in several ways. The Indians are spiritually ashes
(burnt out, lacking the spiritual fuel of belief), arid (lacking the
life-giving waters of faith) or corpses (awaiting the new life that
conversion would provide).

Jesus Christ Inca Valverde is quick to exploit the fusion of
Christian terminology and Inca ritual.

praise him ... scared to hell of him The two comments by
Atahuallpa and Pizarro reveal an interesting contrast of
attitude. The Inca identifies a god with the praise that he can
inspire, the Spaniard with the fear he can instil.

a couple of big ... sky The contrasting characteristics of
gentleness and violence (continued in the next speech) strongly
emphasize the conflicting values and motives of the early
explorers.

shackles and stakes Fetters (for wrists or ankles) associated

with the imprisonment of heretics who were often burned to
death while bound to a stake (wooden post).

twelfth Lord of the Four Quarters Twelfth ruler of the world
(the four quarters are divided by the points of the compass)
Atahuallpa's father, Huayana-Capac was the eleventh Inca
emperor.

Scene 5 The coastal plain of northern Peru, September 1532 (pp.139–42)

The ordinary soldiers express their fears and growing disillusionment with the expedition. De Candia derides the pitiful
Spanish contingent, though Estete will hear nothing against its
patriotic mission. Pizarro arrives, warning Martin of the cruel
and treacherous self-interest of the natural order, though he
fails to undermine the young man's loyalty and is envious of
his innocent optimism. Finally, (the general bluntly explains
his plans to his officers.

we've been had We've been lured here on a false pretext.
starting to rust The humid atmosphere of the tropical forests
has caused the rivets and joints in their armour to rust together.
Strozzi's A famous Renaissance Italian gunsmith.
Any man ... Venetian During the fifteenth and sixteenth
centuries Venice became the richest state in the Mediterranean
as a result of her mercantile empire. The exploitation of
commercial methods gained for Venetians the reputation of
being extreme materialists whose sole objective was the
acquisition of wealth. Estete therefore implies that de Candia
cannot understand anyone whose motivation is a cause or
principle.
Byzantium The eastern counterpart and successor to the
Roman Empire of the west centred on Byzantium or
Constantinople (now Istanbul), which was founded in AD 330
when Constantine I, the first Christian Emperor, moved the
Roman capital to Byzantium. He thus established a distinctive
medieval Eurasian Christian civilization. The empire fell when

Constantinople was captured by the Ottoman Turks in 1453.

immortal part Soul: like Dr Faustus, who traded his soul to the devil for twenty-four years of self-indulgence.

Health? Breeding? Handsomeness An ironic reply: these are qualities that Pizarro obviously lacks.

you'll see a kind of death An inner death, or death of the soul, which has left him without hope.

The eagle rips the condor The condor is a large vulture found in South America. Pizarro places it below the eagle in nature's brutally inevitable hierarchy, in which the strong persecutes the weak: a violent image emphasizing Pizarro's lawless ambition.

gobbets Lumps of raw flesh.

harry me Harass me, challenge me.

you belong You are part of the establishment that accepts and therefore perpetuates traditional values.

crowners Monarchists, those who support the crown.

It's you who ... Generals The religious, political and military institutions of society survive by virtue of the awe and reverence awarded to them.

You own everything I've lost The innocence and idealism of youth. Martin has a romantic faith in the glorious cause that has brought him to Peru: Pizarro's dreams have been shattered by experience.

show it to the Birds A disdainful rebuff. Pizarro has no respect for the hollow authority that Estete tries to wield.

Scene 6 The Andes of northern Peru, October 1532 (pp.143–6)

Pizarro and his men strike into the mountains and begin to explore the Inca empire: a headman explains the country's social structure and system of government. Challcuchima arrives with greetings from his Emperor and is imperiously confronted by Estete. Pizarro, however, accepts the envoy's challenge of a meeting with Atahuallpa high in the mountains, ignoring Estete's cautious advice and leaving him in command of a garrison of twenty men.

road Being a mountainous country, communication in Peru was not simple. However, the Incas overcame geographical obstacles by means of great roads and advanced suspension bridges, which traversed the mountain passes and provided easy access between the capital and the remotest extremities of the empire.

mimosa Or Acacia: a graceful tropical shrub that bears clusters of fluffy yellow balls in spring.

blue glories The Chilean Glory Flower, recognized by its blue trumpet-shaped flowers and pendulous fruit.

net of water 'By a judicious system of canals and subterraneous aqueducts, the waste places on the coast were refreshed by copious streams that clothed them in fertility and beauty.' – Prescott.

toil song The ordinary people of Inca Peru possessed an extensive repertoire of folk songs sung to make their work joyful. Many of these songs, especially those for ploughing and harvest time, were in praise of the sun.

how contented they look Contrary to the traditional European view of work as painful, the natives of Peru were taught that work was gaiety and approached it with whole-hearted pleasure.

I give out to all clothes The ordinary people were organized on an interdependent system similar to that existing in many modern communist states. The ordinary Indians wore a standard uniform and were forbidden any variations (cf. socialist China). Their clothes were issued to them from common stores, and they wore them day and night.

laws of the sun Based on the natural cycle of seasons, which the sun controls, and the work expected of each person at the various months of the year.

maize Commonly known as 'cob' corn: the staple diet of the south American Indians.

age Generation. Just as each month demanded a particular kind of work, so each age group had clearly defined responsibilities in the Incas' highly and rigidly structured society.

always do what they are told An ominously perceptive comment.

Not poor ... All same In a society based on cooperation and strict division of labour 'no man could be rich, no man could be

poor in Peru; but all might enjoy, and did enjoy, a competence'.
– Prescott.

tupu About half an acre. Each family cultivated an allotment of land proportional to its needs and every year family allotments were redistributed to ensure equality of opportunity.

At fifty The Incas had developed a highly sophisticated welfare state which recognized and honoured the work contributed by its individual members, who were guaranteed peace and security in old age.

Here In this place (i.e. Peru).

nothing to covet Since all things necessary for a healthy and comfortable existence were common property under the control of state-appointed officials, ambition, greed and the rebellious or competitive spirit were unknown to the native Peruvians.

light and dark Night and day.

All men are his servants Since the lives of all men are controlled by the influence of the Sun.

great mountains The Andes.

too high for you A taunting challenge.

What I say I do I keep my word. A tragically ironic remark in the light of subsequent events.

I cannot hazard ... officer I cannot risk the life of the King's representative. A sarcastic comment, since Pizarro is conveniently using this reason as a pretext to rid himself of an irritating challenge to his authority.

garrison Probably at the town of Cajas.

Scene 7 Cajas, Peru, October 1532 (pp.146–9)

Pizarro presents the alternative courses of action to his troops and permits them a choice between accompanying his advance or remaining as part of Estete's garrison. After exhortations to suppress their fears with a supreme show of self-assurance, Pizarro's force marches off to win its anticipated spoils constantly observed by Atahuallpa and his increasingly anxious advisers. Old Martin describes the arduous climb high into the mountains and the strengthening of Pizarro's ambitious determination.

three roads Three alternative courses of action.

Who stirs Who steps aside – i.e. to join the Veedor.

chewed up Mutilated: Rodas may also have in mind the cannibalistic reputation of the Indians.

sew us up Repair our uniforms. Rodas was a tailor: Salinas tries to make him feel wanted.

breeches Short trousers fastened below the knee.

dead already Apparently lifeless: the troops have been exhausted by their arduous march.

you're Gods now Survival depends on sustaining the aura of mystery and power that surrounds the invaders. The Spaniards carried three secret weapons – muskets, cannons and horses – the natives thought horses and rider to be one single animal and ran away in terror.

figures from a Lent Procession Unified by a conviction in the cause for which it is fighting, the contingent must conduct itself in the ritualized pageantry of a great religious occasion.

Indifferent! Uncrushable The troops must make a show of proud self-confidence.

cheeseworms Without modern methods of storage, food on the long voyages of early exploration was often contaminated with parasites. The worms here, however, are a powerful symbol of the vulnerability and weakness of Pizarro's men.

village magic Naively simple forms of submissive faith. Meekness is now not only unnecessary but potentially fatal.

pig-boy Popular myth claimed that Pizarro, deserted by both his parents, would have perished had he not been suckled by a sow.

Zaran-Motupe Inca villages in the Andes.

Viracoch'an Atiesi Praise Viracocha – the creator god of the Incas who was, therefore, the father of the Sun (see notes in general introduction).

Sapa Inca! Inca Capac Unique god! sovereign lord.

Caylla, int'i cori Worship the son (cori) of the sun (inti).

Sapa Inca! Huaccha Cuyak Unique god! friend of the humble.

Hands of rock ... nails A powerful metaphorical image which imagines the mountain peaks pointing like figures into the sky with their hard tips of ice (flashing nails).

gashed Slashed, split open (here by the nails). A prophetic image of Atahuallpa's (the sun incarnate) later suffering.

godlings Little gods.

They're vital Not so much as beasts of burden, but as devices to spread terror and panic.

pile Raise up.

lid of the world The highest place on earth.

pull you right out of the sky A powerful expression of Pizarro's soaring ambition: he imagines himself able to overthrow even an acknowledged god.

stay Protect.

Scene 8 The Andes, November 1532 (pp.150–51)

Old Martin describes the extreme suffering of the Spanish soldiers on their climb into the Andes. Villac Umu confronts the force and invites Pizarro to rest at Cajamarca where Atahuallpa intends to meet him.

skittery Nervous, inclined to shy.

pricked Alert, attentive, 'on our toes'.

burning cold Extremes of heat and cold have similar effects on the skin.

cold iron for bones Bones that were stiff and without feeling.

the breath a blade The air was so cold that to inhale was like swallowing a knife.

I am a God Pizarro is playing a game of bluff, convinced that the Incas have a mysterious awe for their invaders that has prevented them from attacking. It is possible that he had not heard of the legend of the white god.

Be still Be quiet! Pizarro recognizes the heresy of identifying himself with divinity, but realizes that it is their main hope of survival.

Outside it is his anger Beyond the limits of the town, where Atahuallpa's forces are in control.

blasphemy Show no reverence towards God – because Pizarro
had said he was a god, too.

usurp Assume, take over what has belonged to another.

Scene 9 Cajamarca, 15 November 1532 (pp.151–4)

Old Martin describes the entry of the Spanish force into the
huge Square of Cajamarca, beyond which was encamped the
Inca army. Pizarro and his companions discuss their predica-
ment and agree to the general's plan of trying to capture the
Inca and hold him hostage. The men disperse to prepare
themselves and their equipment for the ambush.

eucalyptus A gum-bearing tree famous for its beautiful bark.
Its flowers are white, and some varieties have blue leaves.

Ten thousand The chroniclers vary according to the exact
number. Hernando Pizarro (Francisco's brother) estimated the
army to be forty thousand strong.

Brace up Summon up your strength and courage.

One man Atahuallpa, the Emperor. The weakness of his
sophisticated regime was that, by striking at its head, an attacker
could cause the entire organization to crumble (when separated
from the Inca). The officials could no longer administer the
laws, and the elite were disoriented.

It would avoid bloodshed This significant comment strongly
underlines the compassionate nature of de Nizza and the
Franciscan order that he represents. An interesting feature of the
whole debate is the contrasting motives that it reveals.

Venetian Nonsense de Candia has put his finger on the moral
dilemma of the conquest of the Americas. Valverde is
intellectually ill-equipped to answer and avoid the argument by
dismissing it as nonsense. The fact remains that when Pope
Alexander divided the world with a line that awarded Africa
and Brazil to Portugal, and the remainder of the Americas to
Spain, many argued that this was for religious conversion only –
not for conquest and invasion. Many men of the church were
horrified by the cruelty and destruction employed by the

Conquistadors, fearing that such methods would cause the
heathens to abominate the Christian faith.

my job ... far ones de Candia takes de Nizza's spiritual
metaphor literally: being in charge of the artillery he sighted his
guns on the more distant targets.

in file One behind the other, rather than side-by-side.

San Jago Saint James. A favourite patron of the Spanish in
medieval times. The supposed tomb of St James the Great (son
of Zebedee) at Sant Jago de Compostella became the most
famous shrine in Europe in the Middle Ages and the object of
great pilgrimage. The saint's name was subsequently given to
the capital of Chile: Santiago.

A sword Martin's romantic ideals have not made him forget the
essential requirements of his situation.

no mere bar of metal It has a symbolic meaning (the Spanish
cause), as well as a practical purpose.

How remote How distant from Pizarro's own life, which has
been stripped of anything in which he can put his faith.

Holy Virgin The Virgin Mary, mother of Jesus Christ. A
central figure of worship in the Catholic church.

Virgin of the Conception Another title for the Virgin Mary,
whose shrines took several different forms. Diego is, therefore,
threatening – if she does not favour him – to forsake her in one
form, only to worship her in another. A wry joke in a moment of
great danger.

Scene 10 Cajamarca, 15 November 1532 (pp.154–7)

On the eve of battle Pizarro is moved to discuss with his
second-in-command whether, if they die, their sacrifice will
have been worthwhile. De Soto is firm in his allegiance but his
general admits that life has held little meaning for him since
he became aware of the inevitability of death, especially as his
illegitimate background has deprived him of the hope of a
wife and legitimate fatherhood. Time has also stolen from
him his few moments of supreme experience and left him
devoid of feeling. Even so he has continued the search for

something to believe in, and has recently become inspired by contemplating the universal truth that the sun represents. Pizarro feels that the next day's meeting will be the most important of his life.

Sceptres Symbols of the royal power and authority that have also lost meaning for Pizarro.

The Life Today ... Life of Fame Life on earth (mortal existence), life after death (in heaven) and a form of earthly immortality through the survival of his name and reputation.

know it Realize the inevitability of death.

it's all over Life loses all its purpose.

you've been cheated By the realization that all your efforts are fruitless.

having children ... defeating it Because children perpetuate the heritage of their fathers and, by so doing, break down the barriers that time imposes upon individual existence.

badges and barriers Symbols of the orders to which men belong and the institutions founded to protect their identity.

my soul was frostbitten My inner life (capacity for spiritual existence) was stunted before it could grow.

linked together for some great end Formed a coordinated purpose and provided a harmonious meaning.

Everything we feel is made of Time All our experience is conditioned by the portions into which consciousness may at any moment be divided.

becomes maggoty Begins to decompose (eaten by larvae) – since life is part of a cycle of perpetual motion.

something you could pick up Something tangible: a moment cannot be anchored in any specific time scale since it is essentially transient.

You can't escape ... with Time Only by moving with time can you avert the destruction of death.

they wriggle in you anyway The certainty of death is built into you: as life advances, the body comes relentlessly closer to the moment when the maggots will begin their work.

a lust to own their beauty A primitive passion through which man tries to embrace a transcendent experience.

become you and get soiled Become tainted by man's fundamental (original) sinfulness.

purged Cleaned it out.

dandled Bounced, danced.

gurgle i.e. make the first sounds of infant awareness.

I'd find the source of life I would discover life in its purest form, unpolluted by the advances of civilized society.

a strange place of white sand A conception perhaps suggested by the early explorers' picture of the Caribbean islands: a kind of paradise.

fancy Fantasy; imagination.

a heavenly body … perpetual motion de Soto holds the traditional (Ptolemaic) medieval view of the universe in which the earth was thought to be the stationary centre round which the sun and stars revolved.

What if they were wrong A prophetic, ironic query. The views of the astronomer Copernicus (died 1543) were soon to shake the beliefs of medieval man to their foundations by proving that the planets, including the earth, moved round the sun, their permanent fulcrum.

something eternal, against going flesh Something permanent to compensate for man's temporary state of existence.

soothsayer Prophet; diviner of the future.

death … new life Pizarro holds the hope that he may be on the point of discovering a new, spiritual life through which he can brave the certainty of physical death.

Scene 11 Cajamarca, 16 November 1532 (pp.157–60)

The priests lead the soldiers in prayers for deliverance. Hidden in ambush, the Spaniards wait terrified for the Inca to move from his camp. As the sun sets, his army advances on the town where Pizarro's men anticipate their doom. Terror turns into disbelief as the Peruvians lay down their arms and move relentlessly into the trap that has been set for them.

Exsurge Domine 'Rise up, O Lord'. These words occur frequently in the Psalms (Nos. 3, 7, 9, 10, 132) which formed part of the Latin order of divine service based on the Vulgate edition of the Bible.

Deus meus eripe me de manu peccatoris 'O my God, deliver me from the hand of the wicked'. These words seem to be a fusion of parts of two verses from Psalm 140 in which David (just like Pizarro's men) prays for deliverance from his enemies.
Verse 1, Eripe me Domine ab homine malo – Deliver me, O Lord, from the evil man.
Verse 5, Custodi me Domine de manu peccatoris – Protect me, O Lord, from the hand of the wicked.

Many strong bulls ... dust of death These four lines come direct from the revised edition of the English Bible, where in Psalm 22 David complains and prays in distress.
Verse 12, Many bulls have compassed me: strong bulls of Bashan have beset me round.
Verse 13, They gaped upon me with their mouths, as a ravening and roaring lion.
Verse 14, I am poured out like water, and all my bones are out of joint: my heart is like wax; it is melted in the midst of my bowels.
Verse 15, My strength is dried up like a potsherd: and my tongue cleaveth to my jaws: and thou hast brought me into this dust of death.

cleaves Clings, sticks.

plague Fever, disease, historically of tragic epidemic proportions.

glued in a trance Suspended in a hypnotic state.

Don't blink ... too much noise A powerful idea, vividly emphasizing the terrifying tension of waiting.

crawl Creep through the body.

Dread Fear.

They're sweeping the road One of the many extraordinary and elaborate rituals surrounding the Inca to preserve his purity and reinforce his divine identity.

The sun ... stabbed it Peru is now famous for its vividly colourful sunsets. The red glow of the setting sun on this occasion, however, made an even greater impact on the terrified, simple-minded common soldiers.

omen Portent, indication of the future. Domingo sees it unfavourably, as a sign of his own death; unaware that it could also signify the bloodshed that the people of the sun god were soon to suffer.

Apocalypse The Revelation of St John, containing a symbolic prophecy of the final upheaval at the end of the world. The revelation also contains an appeal to Christians to be steadfast in the face of evil and the conviction of God's ultimate victory over Satan.

jeering Laughing derisively.

a miracle Domingo's superstitious faith contrasts sharply with Pizarro's sharp rational analysis of the situation.

in the middle, Fathers In the centre of the town square, Priests.

Oh no, Sir Pizarro's page is unwilling to be separated from his master – according to the laws of chivalry.

San Jago St James (see note, p.62).

Scene 12 Cajamarca, 16 November 1532 (pp.160–63)

Valverde and de Nizza confront Atahuallpa and his followers in the Square of Cajamarca and proclaim the Christian 'Requirement'. The Inca, however, refuses to recognize The Church and angrily throws down the Bible that he has been offered – the sign for the Spaniards to spring from their hiding places and begin the great massacre during which Atahuallpa is taken prisoner.

marracas A kind of rattle made originally from a gourd strung with beads. As a folk instrument it was thought to have magical attributes and accompanied religious rites.

jade Nephrite: a hard, translucent stone of light-green colour.

circlet of plain gold Symbolizing the sun.

killed by men … into the sky Christ's crucifixion and Ascension. There is a deep irony here in that, despite

Atahuallpa's assurance that 'a god cannot be killed', the
Conquistadors will later execute the Inca because of the political
danger that he threatens, just as Christ was crucified on the same
pretext.

See my father The sun (Inti) from whom each Inca claimed
descent.

I will expound As a result of the heated debate over the moral
rights of conquest which profoundly troubled several Spanish
monarchs, a commission was appointed in 1513 at the monastery
of Valladolid. This produced the famous Requirement (here
delivered by Valverde), a proclamation to be read out to the
natives, through interpreters, before Spanish troops opened
hostilities against them thus providing a means for the Indians to
avoid bloodshed by complete and immediate surrender. The
Requirement itself contained a brief history of the world, with
descriptions of the Papacy and Spanish monarchy and of the
donation of the Indies by Pope to King. The Indian audience
was then required to accept two obligations: it must acknowledge
the Church and Pope and accept the King of Spain as ruler on
behalf of the Pope: it must also allow the Christian faith to be
preached to it. If the natives failed to comply immediately, the
Spaniards would launch their attack.

vassal Slave, humble servant.

He gives ... not his Pope Alexander's division of the world
between Spain and Portugal for the purpose of missionary
conquest (see note, p.61).

holds it to his ear Atahuallpa expects to hear 'the word of God'
literally, and is disappointed when the book produces no sound.

Blasphemy Abuse of God's name.

God is angry i.e. Atahuallpa, god of the sun on earth.

stay Withhold, restrain – from attack.

absolve Pronounce you (the Spaniards) free from sin; i.e. the
slaughter they are about to perform has divine justification.

SAN JAGO Y CIERRA ESPAÑA St James and a united Spain.
'Cierra España' had been the battle cry of the crusading Knights
of Castile in their wars to drive the Moors from the Iberian
peninsula. The final victory of this reconquest came when

Grenada fell to the Castillians in January 1492 and Spain became a united Christian country.

quarry Prey: the victim of the hunt.

bellies Swells out.

Revision questions, Act 1

1 Analyse the dramatic function of the first scene of the play and define the important issues it exposes.

2 Put into your own words the main points of the discussion between Pizarro and young Martin at the end of Scene 2.

3 Describe the conflict that exists in the first Act between Pizarro and Estete and explain how it is resolved.

4 Compare and contrast the picture presented in the first act of the two priests who accompanied Pizarro's force.

5 Draw a character sketch of the ordinary soldiers so as to distinguish their differences and reveal their various motives.

6 Explain the dramatic function of Challcuchima and Villac Umu in the first act.

7 Why does Estete believe Pizarro is mad (Scene 5)?

8 Imagine that you are a Spanish soldier. Write an imaginative account, based on the evidence of the text of your journey from Tumbez to Cajamarca.

9 Through close analysis of Scene 10, define and describe the differences in attitude and principle that exist between Pizarro and de Soto.

10 By means of detailed study of the reactions of the men and officers explain the dramatic impact of Scene 11.

Act 2, The Kill. Scene summaries, textual notes and revision questions

Scene 1 Cajamarca, November 1532 (pp.164–5)

Old Martin recalls the horrifying initiation into battle that he experienced at Cajamarca as a young man. De Soto tries to justify to the new Knight the slaughter that has taken place, but Martin feels that they have put the name of Christ to shame. Pizarro awaits reinforcements.

the sun chamber The temple of the Sun at the edge of Cajamarca where Atahuallpa was held under guard.

struts Walks proudly, pompously. A sarcastic comment since young Martin is in a state of collapse.

new spurs In the medieval code of chivalry, the awarding of spurs marked the promotion from squire to knight in recognition of some act of bravery.

we are all eased out of kids' dreams In the process of growing up we all have to leave behind the innocent imaginings of childhood.

who can be ripped ... after Which child can be suddenly brought to face with the brutal realities of the adult world and retain a capacity for love?

The spring of the clock was snapped The driving force behind the structural mechanism of the empire was broken.

not knowing what to do Without a leader the people lost their sense of purpose.

Honourably dead! Not alive and shamed Young Martin still holds on to his belief in what is right. He would prefer a noble death rather than live his life with a shameful conscience.

After he is After the natives have been converted to Christianity.

Stand up ... you Stand up and show your respects to the second-in-command (i.e. de Soto). By recalling the code of conduct, Pizarro is trying to take Martin's mind off his feelings of guilt.

Garrison Left at Cajas with Estete.

Reinforcements The company under Almagro (see 1,2,p.133) which had remained in Panama and was to follow Pizarro after three months.

Scene 2 Cajamarca, November 1532 (pp.165–7)

Pizarro presents himself to Atahuallpa who resents the Spaniard's lack of respect and condemns his treachery. Felipillo, who has been mistranslating the conversation for his own selfish motives, is replaced by Martin as interpreter.

Why does he not kneel The Inca, accustomed to the total humility of his people, cannot comprehend why Pizarro addresses him as an equal.

The Inca ... first came Felipillo tries to exploit his superior knowledge of Quechua to win one of the Inca's wives to satisfy his sexual desires.

He lied to me That Pizarro is no god has been proven to Atahuallpa by his deceitful tactics.

How dare you speak this before my face Atahuallpa's wives were so greatly respected that no one even dared to look them in the face. Felipillo's lustful insolence is, therefore, a serious outrage.

aright Correctly.

I have been on earth thirty and three years There are several references in the play that draw attention to the parallel between Atahuallpa's martyrdom and Christ's sacrifice: the similarity in age represents one such.

That's not true Martin here defends his hero and discreetly chooses not to translate the Inca's words.

privy to Intimate with. Martin participated in their most private discussions.

Scene 3 Cajamarca, December 1532 (pp.168–70)

Martin entertains Atahuallpa with a European card game until Pizarro arrives. The Inca, detecting the general's objective, offers to fill his prison with gold in exchange for freedom. Despite de Soto's warning that the acceptance of such a bargain will not only be dishonest but dangerous, Pizarro thinks the offer will not only satisfy his troops, but also secure their hold on the Emperor, and therefore agrees. As soon as the agreement has been concluded, Atahuallpa orders the gold to be collected from the temples and palaces of Peru.

pyxes Ecclesiastic vessels in which consecrated bread is kept.

What are the poor The cooperative basis of Inca society ensured that each person's needs were supplied.

You can't hide from me Despite the fact that he has been fatally tricked, Atahuallpa is a perceptive and shrewd judge of character.

Two showings of my Mother Moon Two months.

you have no swear to give You cannot enter into this contract: Pizarro had already demonstrated that he could not be trusted.

Refuse, sir. You could never free him De Soto recognizes the political/military necessity of keeping the Inca as a hostage in order to secure the safety of the Spanish force.

General, ... keep it De Soto's traditional code of honour insists that his word is his bond.

I'll never ... same case Brought up on a different set of values where expediency prevails, Pizarro chooses to ignore the distinction between keeping one's word and failing to break it.

niceties Precise logical distinctions.

Alexander The Great (356–23), King of Macedonia (Greece); one of the greatest generals the world has known, conquering the Persians (334), the Egyptians (332), Babylonians (331) and Medes (330). In the summer of 327, Alexander set out to invade India and crossed the Indus in 326.

Tamberlaine (Also spelt Tamburlaine or Tamerlaine.) The Mongol conqueror Timur Lenk (1336–1405). He rose from obscurity as a Scythian shepherd to win the crown of Persia and extend his dominions into Asia. He was chiefly remembered for the barbarity of his conquest and was the hero of Marlowe's play in two parts (1587).

lodestone See 1,1,p.131, and our note p.49.

He has an answer for time He represents a way of reaching beyond the boundaries of time.

touch me Affect me.

Atahuallpa commands Atahuallpa's absolute authority remained unchallenged even in captivity and his orders were as promptly obeyed as before.

walls of pleasure The walls of palaces.

roofs of omen Roofs of shrines and temples.

floors of feasting Floors of banqueting chambers.

ceilings of death Ceilings of tombs.

Quito The capital of the northern province.

Pachacamac Famous shrine and oracle on the coastal desert south of modern Lima.

Cuzco The temple of the Sun: the most important holy place in the Inca empire.

Coricancha The Golden Enclosure: a precinct of the Sun Temple of Cuzco containing many agricultural votive offerings and models.

Vilcanota A river running through the Andes to the north east of Cuzco on whose banks were several important temples including *Colae*.

Aymaraes and Arequipa Temples south of Cuzco on the edge of the coastal plain between Lake Titicaca and the sea.

Chimu A tribal state on the northern coast of Peru centred on Mochica. It was famous for its sophisticated art work, often combining gold with the precious stone, turquoise.

his prison of clouds That which prevents the Inca's light from shining on his people.

Scene 4 Cajamarca, January 1533 (pp.170–76)

Atahuallpa is permitted to exist in his accustomed comfort while the gold is accumulated despite the occasional insult. Valverde questions the Inca on the fundamental principle of his religion, though he finds himself no more capable of understanding than Atahuallpa can comprehend important aspects of Christianity. De Nizza attempts to explain the Christian concepts of sin and love. Meanwhile, Old Martin describes the arrival of the first gold though Pizarro is eager to speed its delivery for fear of a native rebellion. However, the Inca reaffirms his promise and de Soto is sent, at his suggestion, to Cuzco for any sign of unrest. De Nizza determines to convert Atahuallpa and bring to him the blessings of the Christian faith, though the Inca is deaf to his words.

audience his nobles Receive his Lords in formal interview.

vampire birds Bats; popularly believed to be blood-suckers.

ears were hung The Inca nobility were distinguished by golden rings or plugs worn in the ears.

His meals ... had been Atahuallpa was surrounded by a protective screen of women whose task was to supply his every need. The women brought his food in vessels of gold and silver on a mat of thin green rushes: the Inca made his selection and was fed by the hand of one of his ladies.

sweet potatoes Potatoes (oca) originated in Peru and grew there in a profusion of varieties and colours: they were to be Peru's greatest legacy to the world.

What he didn't eat was burnt Anything that had been touched by the Inca had to be burnt, reduced to ashes and thrown into the air since no one was allowed to come into contact with it.

Make me dead with your eyes A taunt for Atahuallpa to demonstrate his divine powers, in which Felipillo does not believe.

saved you from Hell By conversion to Christianity.

Your old God encouraged lust The god of Ecuador whom he worshipped before the arrival of the Conquistadors and their missionaries.

This means ... the Sun's time The logic of this argument covers every eventuality.

First he becomes ... eat him Atahuallpa refers to the consecrated bread received in the sacrament. Reduced to material terms, the ceremony seems laughable since the Inca cannot comprehend its spiritual significance.

My family forbade it many years past During the expansion of the empire in the fifteenth century, the practice of cannibalism, observed by some of the conquered tribes, was banned.

To have his strength Villac Umu thinks physical strength is gained rather than spiritual grace.

This is the devil's tongue The theological debate is becoming too complex for Valverde's simple mind and he has no answer for the paradox that Atahuallpa detects.

the prison of our sin Original sin which conditions our experience of life.

imperfections Faults, weaknesses.

All life is chains Throughout life we are tied to, dependent upon, something.

I need no one Atahuallpa emphasizes his uniqueness, the giver of life upon whom all depends.

he must marry at twenty-five The age at which all marriage took place in Inca society. De Nizza is protesting that love cannot be regulated and commending freedom of choice.

till till he dies Cultivate to the end of his life.

Let God order ... useless to him The significance of love is made meaningless if it is subject to command.

It is a coin ... to rust It is something of great beauty when given freely, but quickly corrodes when bartered.

torn soldier Wounded, scarred soldier.

spent lecher Lecher exhausted by his lust.

fretted Ornamented with decorative patterns.

pesos Spanish gold coins.

wanting in Honesty Lacking truthfulness: insincere.

porters are slow Inca transport was all done by human runners and porters, or by columns of llamas carrying light loads. Despite being an advanced civilization, the Incas had failed to discover the wheel: they used rollers to move vast building blocks, but never invented the wheel spinning on an axis.

both these Villac Umu and Challcuchima.

stiffen Harden his mind.

who whisper revolt The Spaniards began to suspect that the

slow arrival of the gold was merely a delaying tactic to enable a
native army to assemble, attack their invaders and release their
Emperor.

I'll make inspection The historical accuracy of de Soto's
expedition is uncertain at this point. Certainly there was a force
dispatched to Cuzco to speed up the stripping of the temple of
the Sun and another, under Hernando Pizarro, to Pachacamac.
Most authorities agree, however, that de Soto's journey of
reconnaissance set out at a much later time when the situation
had become desperate, only returning, with no evidence of a
native rising, after Atahuallpa had been condemned and
executed.

denies the right to hunger The Inca system of cooperative
welfare ensured that no individual lacked food. de Nizza sees this
as a restriction of liberty.

happiness ... unhappiness Happiness has no meaning since
they are denied the experience of sorrow. This argument is based
on the idea of relativity: we cannot define 'good' unless we
possess a concept of 'evil'.

want Deficiency: poverty – a blessed state as defined in the
Beatitudes.

tomorrow is abolished Hope for a better life in the future is
denied.

Anti-Christ See note p.54

You see now only by his wish You see only by the grace of the
Sun which illuminates the world.

yet try ... for ever Try to look at him too closely and you will
be permanently blinded.

Scene 5 Cajamarca, February 1533 (pp.176–9)

Atahuallpa detects that Pizarro has no faith in his country's
religion and sings him a harvest song whose relevance soon
becomes clear. The two rapidly discover how similar they
are in attitude and origin. Atahuallpa honours Pizarro with
a token of Inca nobility and teaches him a local dance: for
the first time in many years, the general discovers real
pleasure.

Your eyes are smoking wood Your eyes are cloudy (Pizarro cannot see into them).

a harvest song The literal origins of the song have significant metaphorical meaning in this scene. Atahuallpa has stolen the country from his brother with the intention of reaping the harvest of Empire: Pizarro is in the process of robbing the Inca of his land in order to gather its yield of gold.

Huayana Huayana-Capac, Atahuallpa's father, who died around 1526.

Your brother ... my people The Incas did not stress primogeniture. If the eldest or favourite son designated as heir by his father proved weak or incompetent, he was soon deposed by a more aggressive brother in a civil war or palace revolution. Most of the eleven Incas who had ruled up to the time had succeeded only after some struggle.

If in your home ... his crown Atahuallpa puts forward the argument that power should go to those who are worthy of it, not those who inherit it. By rejecting the principle of direct succession he displays a view of life very similar to Pizarro who has no place for the traditional order.

So ... So These repeated words mark an impasse in the dialogue: both leaders recognize the similarities that link them.

To be born ... great man To be born with nothing (illegitimate) encourages men to make themselves famous. In medieval times, bastards were considered a danger to society because, prompted by ambitions of redressing their disadvantage, they were forced to adopt devious tactics.

golden earrings See our note, p.73.

aylu Kingship group or clan: the lineage, through male descent, of the Inca emperor.

litheness Suppleness: fluency of movement.

grotesque Ludicrously ugly and clumsy.

You make me laugh You give me release from the cares of life. Pizarro is elated by the realization that he still has a capacity for spontaneous emotion.

Scene 6 Cajamarca, February 1533 (pp.180–2)

Old Martin recalls the steady growth of the golden ransom and the ravenous greed of the Spaniards. De Soto returns with no evidence of a rising but an amazing description of Cuzco. The soldiers dream of how they will spend their portions and decide to take their share while they can. De Soto, however, halts their lawlessness and restores order.

halberds A spear with an axe-shaped head.

gold inlays The temple of the Sun at Cuzco was lined with slabs of gold.

Welcome back, sir By placing de Soto's return before Atahuallpa's trial, Shaffer increases the dramatic force of Pizarro's dilemma. The general cannot justify the decision to execute the Inca on the grounds of averting a rebellion.

limepit Grave: limepits were used for burning the hair off animal hides and also for disposing of bodies by caustic corrosion.

navel of the earth Like the sun, identified with the source of life.

The garden of the Sun at Cuzco De Soto's description suggests an earthly paradise.

Arabs Arabian horses, famous for their speed.

bash-house Brothel, whore-house.

saddle-backed little fillies Firmly shaped young girls. Salinas's smutty image derives from Diego's longing for a stable of horses, though the blacksmith has another kind of 'riding' in mind!

Andalusia Southern-most province of Spain famous for its ranches (haciendas) which bred horses and fighting bulls.

private property The prospect of vast wealth threatens a state of possessive anarchy which contrasts sharply with the communal satisfaction of the Inca people.

Finding's keepings. That's the law The law of lawlessness, selfish and amoral.

Officers first, then the church Although the officers did take

the lion's share of the treasure, most authorities indicate that the
ecclesiastics received less than the share of the foot-soldiers.
breach Breaking (the law).

Scene 7 Cajamarca, March 1533 (pp.183–8)

De Soto reports that Atahuallpa has fulfilled his part of the
bargain and Pizarro dictates the contract for the Inca's freedom. Atahuallpa is fascinated by the symbolic power of the
words Martin has written but refuses to agree to the safe-
conduct of the whole of the Spanish force upon which he
swears revenge. Pizarro is thus compelled to delay his captive's release and orders the melting down of the gold, harshly
dismissing Martin's pleas to honour the trust that the Inca
has shown. In Pizarro's moment of intense physical and
mental suffering Atahuallpa tries to comfort his captor, but
the old general is torn by a bitter realization of the futility
of life and the inevitability of death for both himself and the
Inca.

hidalgo See note, p.46.
Chica A fermented drink generally made from maize.
on the turn On the point of rebellion.
his honour Pizarro enjoys demonstrating to de Soto, as well as
  Atahuallpa that he has some respect for principle.
Writing, my lord The Peruvians failed to discover writing: the
  closest they came was in the development of mnemonic devices,
  such as coloured beans and dyed threads, to record numerical
  statistics or historical events.
melt everything down According to the chroniclers, the
  melting of gold and silver continued from 16 March to 9 July
  1533.
Italy The centre of European art in the Renaissance period.
tender man Sensitive man. De Soto cherishes the aesthetic
  beauty of much of the treasure that has been accumulated,
  whereas Pizarro recognizes only its material value.
You are the King Through literacy, Martin possesses a power
  that no one else can challenge.

That I do not swear Atahuallpa's interpretation of the agreement is very strict. The relationship he has established with the Spanish general has in no way weakened his desire for revenge.

There is a way of mercy An ironic appeal in the light of the ruthlessness shown by the Conquistadors. In any case, the Incas were harsh rulers when necessary and did not recognize the Christian concept of mercy.

This is not important Justice is absolute and cannot be bent by changing circumstances.

So it's started The process of deception and dishonouring of principle which was predicted.

gloat, gloat Laugh malignantly. Pizarro's shame expresses itself as anger. Not only has his dishonesty been exposed to his deputy but he has been disappointed in the extent of his personal influence over Atahuallpa.

You just can't Pizarro's action is a betrayal of every principle that Martin has been brought up to value.

That was my first and last worship too The moment represents the shattering of Martin's youthful ideals. Pizarro could no longer be a hero in his eyes and no one ever took his place.

easing for it Relief for the pain of the wound.

Death's entered the house The process of destruction has already begun in my body (house).

eyes will curdle Your eyes will coagulate, lose their sparkle.

vicuna wool Animal fibre obtained from the vicuna or alpaca (which, like the llama, is a member of the camel family though without the characteristic hump). The wool is lightweight and high in insulation value. Robes woven of alpaca wool were worn by Incan royalty, thus the animal was subject to protective regulation under their empire.

circles of nature The natural cycle of life and death.

my soul shrugs My inner spirit is uninterested.

nursing ... nurse their young Giving life only to those who will destroy in order to renew life. Pizarro is sickened by the fundamental cruelty of the natural process.

trivial insignificant; unimportant.

seeing Point of view: vision of existence.
cage Prison of life, between birth and death.
go to sleep A euphemistic term for 'to die'.

Scene 8 Cajamarca, June 1533 (pp.188–90)

Old Martin describes the melting down and distribution of the treasure. Estete and de Candia arrive from the garrison but have no news of the reinforcements from Panama. With the possibility of being cut off, the Veedor unsuccessfully attempts to persuade the Venetian to assassinate the Inca.

The masterwork ... fat bars Old Martin's words vividly portray the reduction of works of sophisticated beauty to primitive lumps of metal.
Genoa An important port in the north west of Italy, which became a key naval and commercial base in the Roman empire. It was captured and sacked by the Saracens in AD 936 but recovered to become one of the most powerful and wealthy Mediterranean city states in the fourteenth century.
Milan Capital of the province of Lombardy (northern Italy), gateway to the Alps and strategically situated as a crossing point for trade and communication. Despite the sacking of the Roman city by the Huns under Attila in 452 and its virtual destruction by the Goths in 539, the city re-emerged as one of the most powerful medieval states.
Rome Capital of the Roman empire which, during its decline, was captured and sacked on several occasions – most notably by the Visigoths in AD 410 and the Vandals in AD 455.
Share-out started at once Historical authority indicates that the distribution of gold was not made until 16 July, though the distribution of silver was made on 17 June when the gold was assayed. Shaffer seems, for dramatic impact, to have compressed the historical events at this point.
Pizarro 57,220 gold pesos The quota for a horseman was about 41 kg (90 lb) of gold and 82 kg (180 lb) of silver: foot-soldiers received half this amount. Francisco Pizarro took almost

seven times the Knights' quota: 272 kg (600 lb) gold; 567 kg (1250 lb) silver. De Soto received double: 82 kg (180 lb) gold; 163 kg (360 lb) silver.

fops Dandies: extravagantly dressed courtiers.

I sent runners back to the coast Probably to Tumbez where Almagro's reinforcements were expected to land.

Spanish justice reigns supreme A sarcastic comment. The Spanish had a reputation for an extremely harsh and cruel process of law.

farriers Shoeing-smith responsible for the horses.

coopers Cask-maker and general carpenter.

kick up the tunnel Kick up the backside.

One throat cut i.e. that of Atahuallpa.

It would much relieve the crown It would relieve the King of Spain from being involved in murder.

you have none You have no King. The head of the Venetian state was the Doge, but his authority was limited by a Council of Ministers and Senate.

So the Palace … after all So the House of Justice has a sewer running through it after all. De Candia's words are deliberately coarse. He intends to point out that Spain's apparent show of impartiality and fairness (disinterest) conceals an underlying motive that is disgustingly selfish.

Scene 9 Cajamarca, June 1533 (pp.191–2)

Old Martin recalls the increasing tension and stress in the mountain town. Amid growing rumours of an imminent attack from the Incas, the soldiers gamble away their newly won wealth. When open conflict breaks out, de Soto once more restores order.

frozen boy Paralysed king: impotent, unable to act.

That's just stories That's just rumours – though the Spaniards treated the rumours with the utmost seriousness. Fifty horsemen patrolled constantly and the whole contingent mustered at dawn. Round-the-clock watches were maintained and the men slept in their armour.

the spit The stake, to which one was tied for execution.

Ruminagui (or Ruminavi) one of the three generals – the other two were Challcuchima and Quisquis – who had supported Atahuallpa in the civil war against his brother. Ruminagui had been left in command of the northern province around Quito and was thus in the best position to launch an attack on Cajamarca.

start it all off Mutiny; insurrection.

Scene 10 Cajamarca, July 1533 (pp.193–8)

Amid the growing threat of internal rebellion, de Soto advises his general that honour gives him no alternative course of action but to march out with his army. Pizarro, however, concerned for his reputation, cannot justify the certain sacrifice of his men for the life of his hostage. Even so he is acutely aware of the responsibility he owes to Atahuallpa, and disdains Estete's hollow effort to remind him of his loyalty to King Charles of Spain: Valverde's attempt to remind Pizarro of the evangelical purpose of the expedition merely provokes an impassioned attack on the Church's hypocrisy. De Nizza argues that Peru is not the paradise it might have appeared because its people lack the power of choice which would give them freedom of spirit. Diego arrives to report that he has accidentally killed a soldier in the cause of order and appeals to his general's sense of comradeship. In the face of mounting threats Pizarro, in a defiant gesture, binds himself to Atahuallpa – only to be surrounded by his captains with drawn swords and an ultimatum for the Inca's death.

smoking Smouldering; about to burst into the fire of rebellion.

the whole story lost for always Pizarro maintained at the outset that his main ambition was to win a place in history (see 1,1,p.131).

Whatever I do ... matter The course of events is pre-ordained and whatever I do will not alter it. Pizarro is again expressing his melancholic views of life.

Nothing, if you don't feel it Life is meaningless without the strength of conviction.

I'll not counsel his I won't advise Atahuallpa's execution.

counsel the death of Christ Recommend a course of action which would prevent Christ's teaching being known (because his missionaries would be wiped out).

As good That is as good as certain.

kill or get killed The survival of the fittest: the law of the jungle.

Not for you No mercies will come later for you – because you will suffer the torment of conscience. Despite the fact that throughout this dialogue Pizarro opposes de Soto with largely pragmatic arguments, his second clearly strikes sensitive areas that are very close to the general's thoughts. This is emphasized by the way in which he springs to Atahuallpa's defence when the Crown, Church and Army in their turn put their case for the Inca's execution.

In Peru, I am absolute A supremely arrogant assertion that is not far from the truth, though events later in the scene underline the vulnerability of his position.

There's no choice ... stick by it The concept of choice has no validity if the alternatives involved are equally viable and interchangeable.

the Crown The representative of the King.

Holy Roman vulture Pizarro shows no reverence for his King who was also the Holy Roman Emperor Charles V. He sees him as a bird of prey feeding off the flesh of the efforts of others.

Someone I promised Life Pizarro had already played at being god and the power over life seems to provide him with the meaning he has been seeking.

act out of personal will ... you gave it Only by being a tyrant, an autocrat who recognizes responsibility only to himself can a man free himself from the codes of conduct which constrain conventional authority.

No promise ... a Christian A hollow argument which debases

principle to policy. The argument was put forward on many
occasions to justify Christian cruelty and is here presented as a
loop-hole through which Pizarro might escape from his
conscience.

All your days ... being God You revel in the power that being
the representative of God awards.

milky fingers ... the blade Innocence (covered in mother
milk) of new life is here vividly contrasted with the violence of
death to emphasize the pretended virtue of the Church.

castrates its people Removes the virility, power of its people.

eunuchs Castrated men.

go marketing for Gods Shopping for something to believe in.

And you're ... of corn Are you satisfied to be indistinguishable
and without individual identity?

cheats you sell ... Tomorrow The false principles that you
preach: free will, self denial, hope for the future (the after-life).

pathetic copy Sad, pitiful image.

sepulchre of the soul Graveyard of the soul – because the
freedom of the individual spirit is deliberately suppressed by its
rulers.

sole judge of love Love which is only acceptable on the terms of
the Church's teaching.

spit Spike, wound with a sword.

The coughers spit gold snot A deliberately unpleasant image
to emphasize the extent to which gold has affected every aspect
of life.

The dear old regiment Affectionate loyalty to the idea of
comradeship in arms.

Gang-love Allegiance to a party or social group.

Flag-love Allegiance to a cause, or emblem.

Carlos-the-Fifth-love Devotion to a king and crown.

Jesus-the-Christ-love Devotion to religion.

a commission ... said today Valverde refers to the
Inquisition, an ecclesiastical tribunal established in Spain by the
Pope in 1478 to combat heresy. The first grand inquisitor was the
Dominican Tomas de Torque who came to symbolize the terror
commonly inspired by his courts and gave the Dominican order
a reputation for fanatical ruthlessness. Torture and burning at

the stake were normal treatment for suspected and convicted heretics.

I have no ... nothing I do not recognize your existence. You are not worthy of significance.

Scene 11 Cajamarca, August 1533 (pp.198–201)

Left alone, Atahuallpa confides to Pizarro his profound belief in his own immortality and, despite Martin's protestations, the general finds the idea of a Sun God who is the undying source of life increasingly appealing. At the same time, however, he suspects that Atahuallpa has been laughing at the mental torment he has been suffering and gives a frenzied demonstration of the control he holds over the Inca. Atahuallpa still maintains his supreme faith and persuades the exhausted general to be confessed in the Inca religion. After this, the Inca releases himself and goes to his fate.

They cannot kill me The Incas believed that only their father, the Sun, had the power to decide when their life on earth should end.

Men with no word Men who cannot be trusted to keep faith.

You were choosing me To be king of the Incas.

But Christ's ... is that it The hope of life after death is only acceptable in the form presented in Christian doctrine, is that right?

free of time Since they are immortal, they are not trapped in the confines of time.

To blast ... own persons To force ourselves beyond the limits of time and become timeless, even in our own living forms.

what we know we can't do without What we know to be fundamentally essential to our existence.

sunflowers ... after night Like the flowers, we, at the break of day, turn our faces towards the light of the sun.

We eat you to walk We eat the food that has grown by means of the sun's rays to acquire the strength to walk.

We drink you to sing We drink the water that has been drawn up by the sun into the clouds (forming rain) to lubricate our voices.

Our reins ... we laugh The cares that confine us are lightened by the warmth of the sun to afford us the freedom of laughter.

futile Pointless, ineffectual.

invulnerable Incapable of being wounded, harmed.

I will swallow ... out of me I will embrace death in the knowledge that I will defeat it.

He will ... Believe The unavoidable logic in the necessity of the sun forms the basis of Atahuallpa's supreme assurance.

Take my word Trust in my faith.

put water to your wound Bathe and soothe your mental, as well as physical, torment.

Ichu Andean bunch grass.

Fly up, my bird 'Bird' refers to Atahuallpa who frees himself from Pizarro to face his sentence and death. The bird was a conventional poetic symbol for the soul which was thought to be released from the body after death to fly to heaven: Pizarro hopes his spiritual being (Atahuallpa) will return from death.

Scene 12 Cajamarca, 29 August 1533 (pp.201–4)

Old Martin recounts Atahuallpa's trial and conviction though the Emperor is saved from the stake by agreeing to a last minute baptism. Even so, the Inca faces death appealing to his father, the Sun and is executed with the garrotte. The falling of a rare tear brings Pizarro to a realization that death can bring a release from the burdens of life and, in any case, the very experience of living has a profound intrinsic value. Such thoughts give the old General a new acceptance of the end that lies ahead.

Old Martin concludes by describing the effects of the Spanish regime on the people of Peru, the manner of Pizarro's death and the profound effects that the events that he has described have had upon his own life.

usurping the Throne Wrongly seizing the throne.

killing his brother Huascar.

idolatry Worshipping idols or images.

having more than one wife Polygamy was an accepted part of
the Inca's life. This accusation, like the other three, is based on a
European Christian code of morals that Atahuallpa could not
have been expected to recognize. The Inca had done no harm to
any Spaniard or other person and it is interesting to note that
the charge of secretly planning an armed rescue attempt was not
levelled at him. The immediate outside reaction to the execution
was highly critical and King Charles of Spain was far from
pleased when he first heard the news.

Death by burning The standard form of death for a heretic (see
note on the Inquisition p.84).

His body must stay in one piece If it is to be able to rise from
the dead.

garrottes Spanish for a 'stick'. The method of strangulation
involved placing a stick in the ends of a rope looped around the
neck and twisting until tight.

you never made one of these You never shed a tear.

amber A dull yellow fossil resin used for ornament: Pizarro sees
Atahuallpa's eyes as hard and lifeless.

I lived between two hates Despising idealism yet regretting
the loss of it (see 1,5,p.142).

we know them We can experience them (feelings).

your trust which hunted me Your trust which drove me to
distraction. The word 'hunted' is full of irony since whereas
Pizarro has hunted Atahuallpa physically, the Inca has
relentlessly troubled the general's mind/conscience.

alone make these The values and ideals which sustain us are of
our own creation.

I'm colding too The heat in my body is also cooling in
anticipation of death.

There's nothing but peace to come The release from mortal
suffering that death provides.

slaves shuffle underground In the gold and silver mines.

gorged Surfeited; fed to excess.

distended Swollen with gluttony; bloated.

Son of His Own Deeds Man of his own making.

killed later ... the reinforcements The reinforcements for which Pizarro had been awaiting at Cajamarca eventually arrived and with Diego de Almagro's help the Inca army of the north was defeated. Pizarro and his partner advanced on Cuzco which they entered on 15 November 1533, though they still had to overcome the resistance of the remaining Inca general Quisquis (1534), and suppress the Great Rebellion under the puppet-Inca Manco (1536). Pizarro went on to found Lima, but open rivalry developed between himself and Almagro, whose supporters attacked and killed the ageing General in his palace at Lima on 26 June 1541.

he sat down ... got up again He was laid low by the shattering of his remaining hopes on that morning and never really recovered.

slaveowner Although the Peruvian Indians were originally granted their freedom, their land was divided among the Spaniards from whom they received 'protection' and to whom they were required to provide tribute of local produce and precious metals. This arrangement eventually developed into the system of *Repartimento* under which the Incas were distributed to the Conquistadors to work as virtual slaves.

forty years from any time of hope This reference identifies Martin in age with Pizarro at the time of the conquest. As an old man of about 60, he has looked back to the time when his youthful hopes and ideals were brought to a shocking end.

It put out ... much with age These two sentences depend on a botanical metaphor. Martin compares human life with that of a tree whose blossom has been blasted (blighted) before it could flower, with the result that its fruit (maturity) has never developed that sweetness (peace of mind?) which a more natural process of growth would have allowed.

you did for me ... I've done for you You brought me face to face with reality and now I've told the true story of your campaign.

Revision questions, Act 2

1 Trace the various steps in the development of the relationship between Pizarro and Atahuallpa.

2 Explain the role of Felipillo in this Act (you may also include detail from Act 1).

3 Describe the terms of the agreement between Pizarro and Atahuallpa and explain, in detail, the General's reasons for making it and believing he would not have to honour it.

4 Explain the dramatic significance of Atahuallpa's harvest song in Scene 5.

5 Explain and illustrate why de Nizza changes in attitude during the course of Act 2.

6 Describe the function of young Martin in the second Act of the play.

7 Write a character sketch of de Candia and explain his reasons for defying Pizarro.

8 Explain the appeal that the religion of the Sun has for Pizarro.

9 Make a detailed analysis of the arguments put forward in Scene 10 for and against the assassination of Atahuallpa.

10 Write an imaginative description of Atahuallpa's trial based on the charges that Old Martin recalls at the beginning of Scene 12.

General questions

1 Trace the various levels on which the idea of 'a journey of discovery' operates within the play. Illustrate your answer.

2 Pizarro has lost the savour for life, because his life has been one of rejection. Do you think the play shows that he is justified in rejecting the institutions, values and ideals he has scorned. Give reasons for your conclusions.

3 Describe the attitude of the various members of the expedition, except Pizarro himself, towards Atahuallpa and explain why they adopt their respective positions.

4 Do you consider *The Royal Hunt of the Sun* to be a tragedy? Give reasons for your answer.

5 What impression of human nature do you gain from *The Royal Hunt of the Sun*. Do you think it to be a fair one? Give reasons.

6 Define and explain the concept of 'God' which the various characters in the play maintain. Show how the different definitions supply their individual wants and needs.

7 *The Royal Hunt of the Sun* presents the meeting of two worlds. Give a detailed definition of the nature of these worlds and explain what enables the one to overcome the other.

8 'The author of *The Royal Hunt of the Sun* is no moralist though he does have strong views. He presents his play as a history in order to allow us to judge for ourselves'. Through close analysis of the text, illustrate those views which you think Shaffer presents.

9 'A powerful play of action and suspense.' Illustrate this view by means of a close analysis of three scenes which you think demonstrate these qualities.

10 From the evidence in the text, write a description of the Peru of the Incas and the society which inhabited it.

11 By close analysis of the text illustrate the role that Old Martin plays as narrator and chorus.

12 Make a close study of the different registers of language that Shaffer employs to distinguish the three groups within the Spanish ranks – officers, men and priests.

13 Write character sketches of Pizarro and Atahuallpa and define the differences and similarities that you have observed between them. Use quotations from the text to illustrate your answer.

14 'Spanish general poses as god to impress Inca God King.' Do you think this very brief synopsis of the film of *The Royal Hunt of the Sun* does justice to what is presented in the play? Give reasons for your answer.

15 Pizarro says, 'Dreamers deserve what they get.' Do you think this is a fair comment on the experiences of Young Martin in the play? Give reasons for your answer.

16 What is the significance of the title of the play? Explain and illustrate the various meanings and ideas that emanate from it.

17 Peter Shaffer said that he wrote *The Royal Hunt of the Sun* 'to make colour ... to make spectacle ... to make magic'. Describe the scenes where these qualities are most evident and evaluate to what extent the essential features of the play are diminished in a reading where these qualities must be missing.

18 Write an account of the events contained in the play from Atahuallpa's point of view and attempt to justify his behaviour.

19 'Son of his own deeds.' To what extent is this a fair description of Pizarro? Illustrate from the text and give reasons for your answer.

20 'Love' appears in many guises in the *Royal Hunt of the Sun*. Select, explain and illustrate three of the different forms it takes in the play.

Pan study aids
further titles published in the Brodie's Notes series

W. H. Auden Selected Poetry

Jane Austen Emma Mansfield Park Northanger Abbey Persuasion
Pride and Prejudice

Anthologies of Poetry Ten Twentieth Century Poets
The Metaphysical Poets The Poet's Tale

Robert Bolt A Man for All Seasons

Harold Brighouse Hobson's Choice

Charlotte Brontë Jane Eyre

Emily Brontë Wuthering Heights

Robert Browning Selected Poetry

Geoffrey Chaucer (parallel texts editions) The Franklin's Tale
The Knight's Tale The Miller's Tale The Nun's Priest's Tale
The Pardoner's Tale The Prologue to the Canterbury Tales

Richard Church Over the Bridge

John Clare Selected Poetry and Prose

Samuel Taylor Coleridge Selected Poetry and Prose

Joseph Conrad The Nigger of the Narcissus & Youth
The Secret Agent

Charles Dickens Bleak House David Copperfield Dombey and Son
Great Expectations Hard Times Little Dorrit Oliver Twist
Tale of Two Cities

Gerald Durrell My Family and Other Animals

George Eliot Middlemarch The Mill on the Floss Silas Marner

T. S. Eliot Murder in the Cathedral Selected Poems

J. G. Farrell The Siege of Krishnapur

Henry Fielding Joseph Andrews

F. Scott Fitzgerald The Great Gatsby

E. M. Forster Howards End A Passage to India
Where Angels Fear to Tread

William Golding Lord of the Flies The Spire

Oliver Goldsmith Two Plays of Goldsmith: She Stoops to Conquer;
The Good Natured Man

Graham Greene Brighton Rock The Power and the Glory
The Quiet American

Thom Gunn and Ted Hughes Selected Poems

Thomas Hardy Chosen Poems of Thomas Hardy
Far from the Madding Crowd Jude the Obscure
The Mayor of Casterbridge Return of the Native
Tess of the d'Urbervilles The Trumpet-Major The Woodlanders

L. P. Hartley The Go-Between The Shrimp and the Anemone

Joseph Heller Catch-22

Ernest Hemingway For Whom the Bell Tolls
The Old Man and the Sea

Barry Hines A Kestrel for a Knave

Gerard Manley Hopkins Poetry and Prose of Gerard Manley Hopkins

Aldous Huxley Brave New World

Henry James Washington Square

Ben Jonson The Alchemist Volpone

James Joyce A Portrait of the Artist as a Young Man

Ken Kesey One Flew over the Cuckoo's Nest

Rudyard Kipling Kim

D. H. Lawrence The Rainbow Selected Tales Sons and Lovers

Harper Lee To Kill a Mocking-Bird

Laurie Lee As I Walked out One Midsummer Morning
Cider With Rosie

Thomas Mann Death in Venice & Tonio Kröger

Christopher Marlowe Doctor Faustus Edward the Second

W. Somerset Maugham Of Human Bondage

Arthur Miller The Crucible Death of a Salesman

John Milton A Choice of Milton's Verse Paradise Lost I, II

John Osborne Luther

Alexander Pope Selected Poetry

Siegfried Sassoon Memoirs of a Fox-Hunting Man

George Orwell Animal Farm 1984

Peter Shaffer The Royal Hunt of the Sun

William Shakespeare Antony and Cleopatra As You Like It
Coriolanus Hamlet Henry IV (Part I) Henry IV (Part II) Henry V
Julius Caesar King Lear Richard II Richard III Love's Labour's Lost
Macbeth Measure for Measure The Merchant of Venice
A Midsummer-Night's Dream Much Ado about Nothing Othello
Richard II Romeo and Juliet The Sonnets The Taming of the Shrew
The Tempest Twelfth Night The Winter's Tale

G. B. Shaw Androcles and the Lion Arms and the Man
Caesar and Cleopatra Pygmalion Saint Joan

Richard Sheridan Plays of Sheridan: The Rivals; The Critic;
The School for Scandal

John Steinbeck The Grapes of Wrath Of Mice and Men & The Pearl

Tom Stoppard Rosencrantz and Guildenstern are Dead

J. M. Synge The Playboy of the Western World

Jonathan Swift Gulliver's Travels

Alfred Tennyson Selected Poetry

William Thackeray Vanity Fair

Dylan Thomas Under Milk Wood

Mark Twain Huckleberry Finn

Keith Waterhouse Billy Liar

H. G. Wells The History of Mr Polly

Oscar Wilde The Importance of Being Earnest

William Wordsworth The Prelude (Books 1, 2)

John Wyndham The Chrysalids

W. B. Yeats Selected Poetry

Australian titles

George Johnston My Brother Jack

Thomas Keneally The Chant of Jimmie Blacksmith

Ray Lawler Summer of the Seventeenth Doll

Henry Lawson The Bush Undertaker & Selected Short Stories

Ronald McKie The Mango Tree

Kenneth Slessor Selected Poems

Randolph Stow The Merry-Go-Round in the Sea To the Islands

Patrick White The Tree of Man

David Williamson The Removalists